C-886   **CAREER EXAMINATION SERIES**

This is your
PASSBOOK for...

Water Plant Operator Trainee

Test Preparation Study Guide
Questions & Answers

COPYRIGHT NOTICE

This book is SOLELY intended for, is sold ONLY to, and its use is RESTRICTED to individual, bona fide applicants or candidates who qualify by virtue of having seriously filed applications for appropriate license, certificate, professional and/or promotional advancement, higher school matriculation, scholarship, or other legitimate requirements of education and/or governmental authorities.

This book is NOT intended for use, class instruction, tutoring, training, duplication, copying, reprinting, excerption, or adaptation, etc., by:

1) Other publishers
2) Proprietors and/or Instructors of "Coaching" and/or Preparatory Courses
3) Personnel and/or Training Divisions of commercial, industrial, and governmental organizations
4) Schools, colleges, or universities and/or their departments and staffs, including teachers and other personnel
5) Testing Agencies or Bureaus
6) Study groups which seek by the purchase of a single volume to copy and/or duplicate and/or adapt this material for use by the group as a whole without having purchased individual volumes for each of the members of the group
7) Et al.

Such persons would be in violation of appropriate Federal and State statutes.

PROVISION OF LICENSING AGREEMENTS – Recognized educational, commercial, industrial, and governmental institutions and organizations, and others legitimately engaged in educational pursuits, including training, testing, and measurement activities, may address request for a licensing agreement to the copyright owners, who will determine whether, and under what conditions, including fees and charges, the materials in this book may be used them. In other words, a licensing facility exists for the legitimate use of the material in this book on other than an individual basis. However, it is asseverated and affirmed here that the material in this book CANNOT be used without the receipt of the express permission of such a licensing agreement from the Publishers. Inquiries re licensing should be addressed to the company, attention rights and permissions department.

All rights reserved, including the right of reproduction in whole or in part, in any form or by any means, electronic or mechanical, including photocopying, recording, or by any information storage and retrieval system, without permission in writing from the Publisher.

Copyright © 2024 by
National Learning Corporation

212 Michael Drive, Syosset, NY 11791
(516) 921-8888 • www.passbooks.com
E-mail: info@passbooks.com

PASSBOOK® SERIES

THE *PASSBOOK® SERIES* has been created to prepare applicants and candidates for the ultimate academic battlefield – the examination room.

At some time in our lives, each and every one of us may be required to take an examination – for validation, matriculation, admission, qualification, registration, certification, or licensure.

Based on the assumption that every applicant or candidate has met the basic formal educational standards, has taken the required number of courses, and read the necessary texts, the *PASSBOOK® SERIES* furnishes the one special preparation which may assure passing with confidence, instead of failing with insecurity. Examination questions – together with answers – are furnished as the basic vehicle for study so that the mysteries of the examination and its compounding difficulties may be eliminated or diminished by a sure method.

This book is meant to help you pass your examination provided that you qualify and are serious in your objective.

The entire field is reviewed through the huge store of content information which is succinctly presented through a provocative and challenging approach – the question-and-answer method.

A climate of success is established by furnishing the correct answers at the end of each test.

You soon learn to recognize types of questions, forms of questions, and patterns of questioning. You may even begin to anticipate expected outcomes.

You perceive that many questions are repeated or adapted so that you can gain acute insights, which may enable you to score many sure points.

You learn how to confront new questions, or types of questions, and to attack them confidently and work out the correct answers.

You note objectives and emphases, and recognize pitfalls and dangers, so that you may make positive educational adjustments.

Moreover, you are kept fully informed in relation to new concepts, methods, practices, and directions in the field.

You discover that you are actually taking the examination all the time: you are preparing for the examination by "taking" an examination, not by reading extraneous and/or supererogatory textbooks.

In short, this PASSBOOK®, used directedly, should be an important factor in helping you to pass your test.

WATER PLANT OPERATOR TRAINEE

DUTIES:
   Under direct supervision, undergoes on-the-job training to learn the duties and become qualified as an operator of a water treatment plant; assists in the operation and maintenance of a water treatment plant; performs related duties as required.

TYPICAL WORK ACTIVITIES:
Water/Wastewater Treatment Plant Operator/Trainee:
- Performs study and reading assignments, observes demonstrations, and otherwise learns the techniques of operation and maintenance of a water/wastewater treatment plant;
- Learns and assists in the operation and adjustment of pumps, valves, screens, and related mechanical equipment;
- Learns and assists in the inspection, maintenance and repairs of pumps, valves, screens, and related mechanical equipment;
- Learns and assists in the making of tests to determine chlorine residual;
- Cleans channels, screens, tanks, and other equipment;
- Learns and assists in the preparation and maintenance of activity records and reports;
- Learns and assists in the making of physical tests of water for color, odor and taste;
- Learns and assists in the making of chemical tests of water for alkalinity and residual chlorine;
- Learns and assists in regulating and adjusting chlorinators and other chemical feeders, washing
- filters and settling basins;
- Performs increasingly responsible duties as assigned in the operation and maintenance of a water/wastewater treatment plant.

- **Water Treatment Plant Operator:**
- Operates pumps, valves, motors and related machinery and equipment:
- Performs maintenance work and makes minor repairs to machinery and equipment;
- Records readings of meters, gauges and scales;
- Regulates and adjusts chlorinators;
- Washes filter beds and settling basins;
- Takes samples of water and makes necessary tests for control of plant operation;
- Assists in the instruction of trainees;
- Supervises the work of laborers and other subordinate employees;
- Keeps a log of plant operations and related records;
- Performs custodial duties in connection with maintenance of buildings and grounds.

Wastewater Treatment Plant Operator:
- Starts and stops pumps, motors, air compressors, and related machinery and equipment;
- Makes minor repairs to machinery and equipment;
- Records readings from meters and gauges;
- Treats and disposes of sludge;
- Operates trickling filters;
- Adds chlorine to wastewater;
- Takes samples of wastewater for testing;
- Makes necessary tests for control of plant operation;
- Assists in the instruction of trainees.

SCOPE OF THE EXAMINATION:
The written, test will be designed to measure knowledges, skills and/or abilities in the following areas:

1. **Mechanical aptitude**: These questions test your ability to identify and understand how basic mechanical instruments such as motors and gears work.
2. **Safety practices**: These questions test your knowledge of basic safety practices.
3. **Tools and reading of scales and gauges**: These questions test your ability to recognize or identify basic tools and their common uses and to make accurate readings of various types of dials, scales and gauges.
4. **Elementary chemistry and general science**: These questions test your knowledge of basic processes and concepts in chemistry and general science.
5. **understanding and interpreting written material**: These questions test how well you comprehend written material.
6. **Basic mathematics**: These questions test your ability to use addition, subtraction, multiplication and division to solve basic arithmetic problems that might be encountered in water and wastewater treatment plant operations. Questions may also involve the use of fractions, decimals, averages and percents.

HOW TO TAKE A TEST

I. YOU MUST PASS AN EXAMINATION

A. *WHAT EVERY CANDIDATE SHOULD KNOW*

Examination applicants often ask us for help in preparing for the written test. What can I study in advance? What kinds of questions will be asked? How will the test be given? How will the papers be graded?

As an applicant for a civil service examination, you may be wondering about some of these things. Our purpose here is to suggest effective methods of advance study and to describe civil service examinations.

Your chances for success on this examination can be increased if you know how to prepare. Those "pre-examination jitters" can be reduced if you know what to expect. You can even experience an adventure in good citizenship if you know why civil service exams are given.

B. *WHY ARE CIVIL SERVICE EXAMINATIONS GIVEN?*

Civil service examinations are important to you in two ways. As a citizen, you want public jobs filled by employees who know how to do their work. As a job seeker, you want a fair chance to compete for that job on an equal footing with other candidates. The best-known means of accomplishing this two-fold goal is the competitive examination.

Exams are widely publicized throughout the nation. They may be administered for jobs in federal, state, city, municipal, town or village governments or agencies.

Any citizen may apply, with some limitations, such as the age or residence of applicants. Your experience and education may be reviewed to see whether you meet the requirements for the particular examination. When these requirements exist, they are reasonable and applied consistently to all applicants. Thus, a competitive examination may cause you some uneasiness now, but it is your privilege and safeguard.

C. *HOW ARE CIVIL SERVICE EXAMS DEVELOPED?*

Examinations are carefully written by trained technicians who are specialists in the field known as "psychological measurement," in consultation with recognized authorities in the field of work that the test will cover. These experts recommend the subject matter areas or skills to be tested; only those knowledges or skills important to your success on the job are included. The most reliable books and source materials available are used as references. Together, the experts and technicians judge the difficulty level of the questions.

Test technicians know how to phrase questions so that the problem is clearly stated. Their ethics do not permit "trick" or "catch" questions. Questions may have been tried out on sample groups, or subjected to statistical analysis, to determine their usefulness.

Written tests are often used in combination with performance tests, ratings of training and experience, and oral interviews. All of these measures combine to form the best-known means of finding the right person for the right job.

II. HOW TO PASS THE WRITTEN TEST

A. NATURE OF THE EXAMINATION

To prepare intelligently for civil service examinations, you should know how they differ from school examinations you have taken. In school you were assigned certain definite pages to read or subjects to cover. The examination questions were quite detailed and usually emphasized memory. Civil service exams, on the other hand, try to discover your present ability to perform the duties of a position, plus your potentiality to learn these duties. In other words, a civil service exam attempts to predict how successful you will be. Questions cover such a broad area that they cannot be as minute and detailed as school exam questions.

In the public service similar kinds of work, or positions, are grouped together in one "class." This process is known as *position-classification*. All the positions in a class are paid according to the salary range for that class. One class title covers all of these positions, and they are all tested by the same examination.

B. FOUR BASIC STEPS

1) Study the announcement

How, then, can you know what subjects to study? Our best answer is: "Learn as much as possible about the class of positions for which you've applied." The exam will test the knowledge, skills and abilities needed to do the work.

Your most valuable source of information about the position you want is the official exam announcement. This announcement lists the training and experience qualifications. Check these standards and apply only if you come reasonably close to meeting them.

The brief description of the position in the examination announcement offers some clues to the subjects which will be tested. Think about the job itself. Review the duties in your mind. Can you perform them, or are there some in which you are rusty? Fill in the blank spots in your preparation.

Many jurisdictions preview the written test in the exam announcement by including a section called "Knowledge and Abilities Required," "Scope of the Examination," or some similar heading. Here you will find out specifically what fields will be tested.

2) Review your own background

Once you learn in general what the position is all about, and what you need to know to do the work, ask yourself which subjects you already know fairly well and which need improvement. You may wonder whether to concentrate on improving your strong areas or on building some background in your fields of weakness. When the announcement has specified "some knowledge" or "considerable knowledge," or has used adjectives like "beginning principles of…" or "advanced … methods," you can get a clue as to the number and difficulty of questions to be asked in any given field. More questions, and hence broader coverage, would be included for those subjects which are more important in the work. Now weigh your strengths and weaknesses against the job requirements and prepare accordingly.

3) Determine the level of the position

Another way to tell how intensively you should prepare is to understand the level of the job for which you are applying. Is it the entering level? In other words, is this the position in which beginners in a field of work are hired? Or is it an intermediate or advanced level? Sometimes this is indicated by such words as "Junior" or "Senior" in the class title. Other jurisdictions use Roman numerals to designate the level – Clerk I, Clerk II, for example. The word "Supervisor" sometimes appears in the title. If the level is not indicated by the title, check the description of duties. Will you be working under very close supervision, or will you have responsibility for independent decisions in this work?

4) Choose appropriate study materials

Now that you know the subjects to be examined and the relative amount of each subject to be covered, you can choose suitable study materials. For beginning level jobs, or even advanced ones, if you have a pronounced weakness in some aspect of your training, read a modern, standard textbook in that field. Be sure it is up to date and has general coverage. Such books are normally available at your library, and the librarian will be glad to help you locate one. For entry-level positions, questions of appropriate difficulty are chosen – neither highly advanced questions, nor those too simple. Such questions require careful thought but not advanced training.

If the position for which you are applying is technical or advanced, you will read more advanced, specialized material. If you are already familiar with the basic principles of your field, elementary textbooks would waste your time. Concentrate on advanced textbooks and technical periodicals. Think through the concepts and review difficult problems in your field.

These are all general sources. You can get more ideas on your own initiative, following these leads. For example, training manuals and publications of the government agency which employs workers in your field can be useful, particularly for technical and professional positions. A letter or visit to the government department involved may result in more specific study suggestions, and certainly will provide you with a more definite idea of the exact nature of the position you are seeking.

III. KINDS OF TESTS

Tests are used for purposes other than measuring knowledge and ability to perform specified duties. For some positions, it is equally important to test ability to make adjustments to new situations or to profit from training. In others, basic mental abilities not dependent on information are essential. Questions which test these things may not appear as pertinent to the duties of the position as those which test for knowledge and information. Yet they are often highly important parts of a fair examination. For very general questions, it is almost impossible to help you direct your study efforts. What we can do is to point out some of the more common of these general abilities needed in public service positions and describe some typical questions.

1) General information

Broad, general information has been found useful for predicting job success in some kinds of work. This is tested in a variety of ways, from vocabulary lists to questions about current events. Basic background in some field of work, such as sociology or economics, may be sampled in a group of questions. Often these are principles which have become familiar to most persons through exposure rather than through formal training. It is difficult to advise you how to study for these questions; being alert to the world around you is our best suggestion.

2) Verbal ability

An example of an ability needed in many positions is verbal or language ability. Verbal ability is, in brief, the ability to use and understand words. Vocabulary and grammar tests are typical measures of this ability. Reading comprehension or paragraph interpretation questions are common in many kinds of civil service tests. You are given a paragraph of written material and asked to find its central meaning.

3) Numerical ability

Number skills can be tested by the familiar arithmetic problem, by checking paired lists of numbers to see which are alike and which are different, or by interpreting charts and graphs. In the latter test, a graph may be printed in the test booklet which you are asked to use as the basis for answering questions.

4) Observation

A popular test for law-enforcement positions is the observation test. A picture is shown to you for several minutes, then taken away. Questions about the picture test your ability to observe both details and larger elements.

5) Following directions

In many positions in the public service, the employee must be able to carry out written instructions dependably and accurately. You may be given a chart with several columns, each column listing a variety of information. The questions require you to carry out directions involving the information given in the chart.

6) Skills and aptitudes

Performance tests effectively measure some manual skills and aptitudes. When the skill is one in which you are trained, such as typing or shorthand, you can practice. These tests are often very much like those given in business school or high school courses. For many of the other skills and aptitudes, however, no short-time preparation can be made. Skills and abilities natural to you or that you have developed throughout your lifetime are being tested.

Many of the general questions just described provide all the data needed to answer the questions and ask you to use your reasoning ability to find the answers. Your best preparation for these tests, as well as for tests of facts and ideas, is to be at your physical and mental best. You, no doubt, have your own methods of getting into an exam-taking mood and keeping "in shape." The next section lists some ideas on this subject.

IV. KINDS OF QUESTIONS

Only rarely is the "essay" question, which you answer in narrative form, used in civil service tests. Civil service tests are usually of the short-answer type. Full instructions for answering these questions will be given to you at the examination. But in case this is your first experience with short-answer questions and separate answer sheets, here is what you need to know:

1) Multiple-choice Questions

Most popular of the short-answer questions is the "multiple choice" or "best answer" question. It can be used, for example, to test for factual knowledge, ability to solve problems or judgment in meeting situations found at work.

A multiple-choice question is normally one of three types—
- It can begin with an incomplete statement followed by several possible endings. You are to find the one ending which *best* completes the statement, although some of the others may not be entirely wrong.
- It can also be a complete statement in the form of a question which is answered by choosing one of the statements listed.

- It can be in the form of a problem – again you select the best answer.

Here is an example of a multiple-choice question with a discussion which should give you some clues as to the method for choosing the right answer:

When an employee has a complaint about his assignment, the action which will *best* help him overcome his difficulty is to
   A. discuss his difficulty with his coworkers
   B. take the problem to the head of the organization
   C. take the problem to the person who gave him the assignment
   D. say nothing to anyone about his complaint

In answering this question, you should study each of the choices to find which is best. Consider choice "A" – Certainly an employee may discuss his complaint with fellow employees, but no change or improvement can result, and the complaint remains unresolved. Choice "B" is a poor choice since the head of the organization probably does not know what assignment you have been given, and taking your problem to him is known as "going over the head" of the supervisor. The supervisor, or person who made the assignment, is the person who can clarify it or correct any injustice. Choice "C" is, therefore, correct. To say nothing, as in choice "D," is unwise. Supervisors have and interest in knowing the problems employees are facing, and the employee is seeking a solution to his problem.

2) True/False Questions

The "true/false" or "right/wrong" form of question is sometimes used. Here a complete statement is given. Your job is to decide whether the statement is right or wrong.

SAMPLE: A roaming cell-phone call to a nearby city costs less than a non-roaming call to a distant city.

This statement is wrong, or false, since roaming calls are more expensive.
This is not a complete list of all possible question forms, although most of the others are variations of these common types. You will always get complete directions for answering questions. Be sure you understand *how* to mark your answers – ask questions until you do.

V. RECORDING YOUR ANSWERS

Computer terminals are used more and more today for many different kinds of exams.
For an examination with very few applicants, you may be told to record your answers in the test booklet itself. Separate answer sheets are much more common. If this separate answer sheet is to be scored by machine – and this is often the case – it is highly important that you mark your answers correctly in order to get credit.
An electronic scoring machine is often used in civil service offices because of the speed with which papers can be scored. Machine-scored answer sheets must be marked with a pencil, which will be given to you. This pencil has a high graphite content which responds to the electronic scoring machine. As a matter of fact, stray dots may register as answers, so do not let your pencil rest on the answer sheet while you are pondering the correct answer. Also, if your pencil lead breaks or is otherwise defective, ask for another.

Since the answer sheet will be dropped in a slot in the scoring machine, be careful not to bend the corners or get the paper crumpled.

The answer sheet normally has five vertical columns of numbers, with 30 numbers to a column. These numbers correspond to the question numbers in your test booklet. After each number, going across the page are four or five pairs of dotted lines. These short dotted lines have small letters or numbers above them. The first two pairs may also have a "T" or "F" above the letters. This indicates that the first two pairs only are to be used if the questions are of the true-false type. If the questions are multiple choice, disregard the "T" and "F" and pay attention only to the small letters or numbers.

Answer your questions in the manner of the sample that follows:

32. The largest city in the United States is
 A. Washington, D.C.
 B. New York City
 C. Chicago
 D. Detroit
 E. San Francisco

1) Choose the answer you think is best. (New York City is the largest, so "B" is correct.)
2) Find the row of dotted lines numbered the same as the question you are answering. (Find row number 32)
3) Find the pair of dotted lines corresponding to the answer. (Find the pair of lines under the mark "B.")
4) Make a solid black mark between the dotted lines.

VI. BEFORE THE TEST

Common sense will help you find procedures to follow to get ready for an examination. Too many of us, however, overlook these sensible measures. Indeed, nervousness and fatigue have been found to be the most serious reasons why applicants fail to do their best on civil service tests. Here is a list of reminders:

- Begin your preparation early – Don't wait until the last minute to go scurrying around for books and materials or to find out what the position is all about.
- Prepare continuously – An hour a night for a week is better than an all-night cram session. This has been definitely established. What is more, a night a week for a month will return better dividends than crowding your study into a shorter period of time.
- Locate the place of the exam – You have been sent a notice telling you when and where to report for the examination. If the location is in a different town or otherwise unfamiliar to you, it would be well to inquire the best route and learn something about the building.
- Relax the night before the test – Allow your mind to rest. Do not study at all that night. Plan some mild recreation or diversion; then go to bed early and get a good night's sleep.
- Get up early enough to make a leisurely trip to the place for the test – This way unforeseen events, traffic snarls, unfamiliar buildings, etc. will not upset you.
- Dress comfortably – A written test is not a fashion show. You will be known by number and not by name, so wear something comfortable.

- Leave excess paraphernalia at home – Shopping bags and odd bundles will get in your way. You need bring only the items mentioned in the official notice you received; usually everything you need is provided. Do not bring reference books to the exam. They will only confuse those last minutes and be taken away from you when in the test room.
- Arrive somewhat ahead of time – If because of transportation schedules you must get there very early, bring a newspaper or magazine to take your mind off yourself while waiting.
- Locate the examination room – When you have found the proper room, you will be directed to the seat or part of the room where you will sit. Sometimes you are given a sheet of instructions to read while you are waiting. Do not fill out any forms until you are told to do so; just read them and be prepared.
- Relax and prepare to listen to the instructions
- If you have any physical problem that may keep you from doing your best, be sure to tell the test administrator. If you are sick or in poor health, you really cannot do your best on the exam. You can come back and take the test some other time.

VII. AT THE TEST

The day of the test is here and you have the test booklet in your hand. The temptation to get going is very strong. Caution! There is more to success than knowing the right answers. You must know how to identify your papers and understand variations in the type of short-answer question used in this particular examination. Follow these suggestions for maximum results from your efforts:

1) Cooperate with the monitor

The test administrator has a duty to create a situation in which you can be as much at ease as possible. He will give instructions, tell you when to begin, check to see that you are marking your answer sheet correctly, and so on. He is not there to guard you, although he will see that your competitors do not take unfair advantage. He wants to help you do your best.

2) Listen to all instructions

Don't jump the gun! Wait until you understand all directions. In most civil service tests you get more time than you need to answer the questions. So don't be in a hurry. Read each word of instructions until you clearly understand the meaning. Study the examples, listen to all announcements and follow directions. Ask questions if you do not understand what to do.

3) Identify your papers

Civil service exams are usually identified by number only. You will be assigned a number; you must not put your name on your test papers. Be sure to copy your number correctly. Since more than one exam may be given, copy your exact examination title.

4) Plan your time

Unless you are told that a test is a "speed" or "rate of work" test, speed itself is usually not important. Time enough to answer all the questions will be provided, but this does not mean that you have all day. An overall time limit has been set. Divide the total time (in minutes) by the number of questions to determine the approximate time you have for each question.

5) Do not linger over difficult questions

If you come across a difficult question, mark it with a paper clip (useful to have along) and come back to it when you have been through the booklet. One caution if you do this – be sure to skip a number on your answer sheet as well. Check often to be sure that you have not lost your place and that you are marking in the row numbered the same as the question you are answering.

6) Read the questions

Be sure you know what the question asks! Many capable people are unsuccessful because they failed to *read* the questions correctly.

7) Answer all questions

Unless you have been instructed that a penalty will be deducted for incorrect answers, it is better to guess than to omit a question.

8) Speed tests

It is often better NOT to guess on speed tests. It has been found that on timed tests people are tempted to spend the last few seconds before time is called in marking answers at random – without even reading them – in the hope of picking up a few extra points. To discourage this practice, the instructions may warn you that your score will be "corrected" for guessing. That is, a penalty will be applied. The incorrect answers will be deducted from the correct ones, or some other penalty formula will be used.

9) Review your answers

If you finish before time is called, go back to the questions you guessed or omitted to give them further thought. Review other answers if you have time.

10) Return your test materials

If you are ready to leave before others have finished or time is called, take ALL your materials to the monitor and leave quietly. Never take any test material with you. The monitor can discover whose papers are not complete, and taking a test booklet may be grounds for disqualification.

VIII. EXAMINATION TECHNIQUES

1) Read the general instructions carefully. These are usually printed on the first page of the exam booklet. As a rule, these instructions refer to the timing of the examination; the fact that you should not start work until the signal and must stop work at a signal, etc. If there are any *special* instructions, such as a choice of questions to be answered, make sure that you note this instruction carefully.

2) When you are ready to start work on the examination, that is as soon as the signal has been given, read the instructions to each question booklet, underline any key words or phrases, such as *least, best, outline, describe* and the like. In this way you will tend to answer as requested rather than discover on reviewing your paper that you *listed without describing*, that you selected the *worst* choice rather than the *best* choice, etc.

3) If the examination is of the objective or multiple-choice type – that is, each question will also give a series of possible answers: A, B, C or D, and you are called upon to select the best answer and write the letter next to that answer on your answer paper – it is advisable to start answering each question in turn. There may be anywhere from 50 to 100 such questions in the three or four hours allotted and you can see how much time would be taken if you read through all the questions before beginning to answer any. Furthermore, if you come across a question or group of questions which you know would be difficult to answer, it would undoubtedly affect your handling of all the other questions.

4) If the examination is of the essay type and contains but a few questions, it is a moot point as to whether you should read all the questions before starting to answer any one. Of course, if you are given a choice – say five out of seven and the like – then it is essential to read all the questions so you can eliminate the two that are most difficult. If, however, you are asked to answer all the questions, there may be danger in trying to answer the easiest one first because you may find that you will spend too much time on it. The best technique is to answer the first question, then proceed to the second, etc.

5) Time your answers. Before the exam begins, write down the time it started, then add the time allowed for the examination and write down the time it must be completed, then divide the time available somewhat as follows:
    - If 3-1/2 hours are allowed, that would be 210 minutes. If you have 80 objective-type questions, that would be an average of 2-1/2 minutes per question. Allow yourself no more than 2 minutes per question, or a total of 160 minutes, which will permit about 50 minutes to review.
    - If for the time allotment of 210 minutes there are 7 essay questions to answer, that would average about 30 minutes a question. Give yourself only 25 minutes per question so that you have about 35 minutes to review.

6) The most important instruction is to *read each question* and make sure you know what is wanted. The second most important instruction is to *time yourself properly* so that you answer every question. The third most important instruction is to *answer every question*. Guess if you have to but include something for each question. Remember that you will receive no credit for a blank and will probably receive some credit if you write something in answer to an essay question. If you guess a letter – say "B" for a multiple-choice question – you may have guessed right. If you leave a blank as an answer to a multiple-choice question, the examiners may respect your feelings but it will not add a point to your score. Some exams may penalize you for wrong answers, so in such cases *only*, you may not want to guess unless you have some basis for your answer.

7) Suggestions
    a. Objective-type questions
        1. Examine the question booklet for proper sequence of pages and questions
        2. Read all instructions carefully
        3. Skip any question which seems too difficult; return to it after all other questions have been answered
        4. Apportion your time properly; do not spend too much time on any single question or group of questions

5. Note and underline key words – *all, most, fewest, least, best, worst, same, opposite*, etc.
6. Pay particular attention to negatives
7. Note unusual option, e.g., unduly long, short, complex, different or similar in content to the body of the question
8. Observe the use of "hedging" words – *probably, may, most likely*, etc.
9. Make sure that your answer is put next to the same number as the question
10. Do not second-guess unless you have good reason to believe the second answer is definitely more correct
11. Cross out original answer if you decide another answer is more accurate; do not erase until you are ready to hand your paper in
12. Answer all questions; guess unless instructed otherwise
13. Leave time for review

b. Essay questions
   1. Read each question carefully
   2. Determine exactly what is wanted. Underline key words or phrases.
   3. Decide on outline or paragraph answer
   4. Include many different points and elements unless asked to develop any one or two points or elements
   5. Show impartiality by giving pros and cons unless directed to select one side only
   6. Make and write down any assumptions you find necessary to answer the questions
   7. Watch your English, grammar, punctuation and choice of words
   8. Time your answers; don't crowd material

8) Answering the essay question

Most essay questions can be answered by framing the specific response around several key words or ideas. Here are a few such key words or ideas:

M's: manpower, materials, methods, money, management
P's: purpose, program, policy, plan, procedure, practice, problems, pitfalls, personnel, public relations

   a. Six basic steps in handling problems:
      1. Preliminary plan and background development
      2. Collect information, data and facts
      3. Analyze and interpret information, data and facts
      4. Analyze and develop solutions as well as make recommendations
      5. Prepare report and sell recommendations
      6. Install recommendations and follow up effectiveness

   b. Pitfalls to avoid
      1. *Taking things for granted* – A statement of the situation does not necessarily imply that each of the elements is necessarily true; for example, a complaint may be invalid and biased so that all that can be taken for granted is that a complaint has been registered

2. *Considering only one side of a situation* – Wherever possible, indicate several alternatives and then point out the reasons you selected the best one
3. *Failing to indicate follow up* – Whenever your answer indicates action on your part, make certain that you will take proper follow-up action to see how successful your recommendations, procedures or actions turn out to be
4. *Taking too long in answering any single question* – Remember to time your answers properly

IX. AFTER THE TEST

Scoring procedures differ in detail among civil service jurisdictions although the general principles are the same. Whether the papers are hand-scored or graded by machine we have described, they are nearly always graded by number. That is, the person who marks the paper knows only the number – never the name – of the applicant. Not until all the papers have been graded will they be matched with names. If other tests, such as training and experience or oral interview ratings have been given, scores will be combined. Different parts of the examination usually have different weights. For example, the written test might count 60 percent of the final grade, and a rating of training and experience 40 percent. In many jurisdictions, veterans will have a certain number of points added to their grades.

After the final grade has been determined, the names are placed in grade order and an eligible list is established. There are various methods for resolving ties between those who get the same final grade – probably the most common is to place first the name of the person whose application was received first. Job offers are made from the eligible list in the order the names appear on it. You will be notified of your grade and your rank as soon as all these computations have been made. This will be done as rapidly as possible.

People who are found to meet the requirements in the announcement are called "eligibles." Their names are put on a list of eligible candidates. An eligible's chances of getting a job depend on how high he stands on this list and how fast agencies are filling jobs from the list.

When a job is to be filled from a list of eligibles, the agency asks for the names of people on the list of eligibles for that job. When the civil service commission receives this request, it sends to the agency the names of the three people highest on this list. Or, if the job to be filled has specialized requirements, the office sends the agency the names of the top three persons who meet these requirements from the general list.

The appointing officer makes a choice from among the three people whose names were sent to him. If the selected person accepts the appointment, the names of the others are put back on the list to be considered for future openings.

That is the rule in hiring from all kinds of eligible lists, whether they are for typist, carpenter, chemist, or something else. For every vacancy, the appointing officer has his choice of any one of the top three eligibles on the list. This explains why the person whose name is on top of the list sometimes does not get an appointment when some of the persons lower on the list do. If the appointing officer chooses the second or third eligible, the No. 1 eligible does not get a job at once, but stays on the list until he is appointed or the list is terminated.

X. HOW TO PASS THE INTERVIEW TEST

The examination for which you applied requires an oral interview test. You have already taken the written test and you are now being called for the interview test – the final part of the formal examination.

You may think that it is not possible to prepare for an interview test and that there are no procedures to follow during an interview. Our purpose is to point out some things you can do in advance that will help you and some good rules to follow and pitfalls to avoid while you are being interviewed.

What is an interview supposed to test?

The written examination is designed to test the technical knowledge and competence of the candidate; the oral is designed to evaluate intangible qualities, not readily measured otherwise, and to establish a list showing the relative fitness of each candidate – as measured against his competitors – for the position sought. Scoring is not on the basis of "right" and "wrong," but on a sliding scale of values ranging from "not passable" to "outstanding." As a matter of fact, it is possible to achieve a relatively low score without a single "incorrect" answer because of evident weakness in the qualities being measured.

Occasionally, an examination may consist entirely of an oral test – either an individual or a group oral. In such cases, information is sought concerning the technical knowledges and abilities of the candidate, since there has been no written examination for this purpose. More commonly, however, an oral test is used to supplement a written examination.

Who conducts interviews?

The composition of oral boards varies among different jurisdictions. In nearly all, a representative of the personnel department serves as chairman. One of the members of the board may be a representative of the department in which the candidate would work. In some cases, "outside experts" are used, and, frequently, a businessman or some other representative of the general public is asked to serve. Labor and management or other special groups may be represented. The aim is to secure the services of experts in the appropriate field.

However the board is composed, it is a good idea (and not at all improper or unethical) to ascertain in advance of the interview who the members are and what groups they represent. When you are introduced to them, you will have some idea of their backgrounds and interests, and at least you will not stutter and stammer over their names.

What should be done before the interview?

While knowledge about the board members is useful and takes some of the surprise element out of the interview, there is other preparation which is more substantive. It *is* possible to prepare for an oral interview – in several ways:

1) Keep a copy of your application and review it carefully before the interview

This may be the only document before the oral board, and the starting point of the interview. Know what education and experience you have listed there, and the sequence and dates of all of it. Sometimes the board will ask you to review the highlights of your experience for them; you should not have to hem and haw doing it.

2) Study the class specification and the examination announcement

Usually, the oral board has one or both of these to guide them. The qualities, characteristics or knowledges required by the position sought are stated in these documents. They offer valuable clues as to the nature of the oral interview. For example, if the job involves supervisory responsibilities, the announcement will usually indicate that knowledge of modern supervisory methods and the qualifications of the candidate as a supervisor will be tested. If so, you can expect such questions, frequently in the form of a hypothetical situation which you are expected to solve. NEVER go into an oral without knowledge of the duties and responsibilities of the job you seek.

3) Think through each qualification required

Try to visualize the kind of questions you would ask if you were a board member. How well could you answer them? Try especially to appraise your own knowledge and background in each area, *measured against the job sought*, and identify any areas in which you are weak. Be critical and realistic – do not flatter yourself.

4) Do some general reading in areas in which you feel you may be weak

For example, if the job involves supervision and your past experience has NOT, some general reading in supervisory methods and practices, particularly in the field of human relations, might be useful. Do NOT study agency procedures or detailed manuals. The oral board will be testing your understanding and capacity, not your memory.

5) Get a good night's sleep and watch your general health and mental attitude

You will want a clear head at the interview. Take care of a cold or any other minor ailment, and of course, no hangovers.

What should be done on the day of the interview?

Now comes the day of the interview itself. Give yourself plenty of time to get there. Plan to arrive somewhat ahead of the scheduled time, particularly if your appointment is in the fore part of the day. If a previous candidate fails to appear, the board might be ready for you a bit early. By early afternoon an oral board is almost invariably behind schedule if there are many candidates, and you may have to wait. Take along a book or magazine to read, or your application to review, but leave any extraneous material in the waiting room when you go in for your interview. In any event, relax and compose yourself.

The matter of dress is important. The board is forming impressions about you – from your experience, your manners, your attitude, and your appearance. Give your personal appearance careful attention. Dress your best, but not your flashiest. Choose conservative, appropriate clothing, and be sure it is immaculate. This is a business interview, and your appearance should indicate that you regard it as such. Besides, being well groomed and properly dressed will help boost your confidence.

Sooner or later, someone will call your name and escort you into the interview room. *This is it.* From here on you are on your own. It is too late for any more preparation. But remember, you asked for this opportunity to prove your fitness, and you are here because your request was granted.

What happens when you go in?

The usual sequence of events will be as follows: The clerk (who is often the board stenographer) will introduce you to the chairman of the oral board, who will introduce you to the other members of the board. Acknowledge the introductions before you sit down. Do not be surprised if you find a microphone facing you or a stenotypist sitting by. Oral interviews are usually recorded in the event of an appeal or other review.

Usually the chairman of the board will open the interview by reviewing the highlights of your education and work experience from your application – primarily for the benefit of the other members of the board, as well as to get the material into the record. Do not interrupt or comment unless there is an error or significant misinterpretation; if that is the case, do not hesitate. But do not quibble about insignificant matters. Also, he will usually ask you some question about your education, experience or your present job – partly to get you to start talking and to establish the interviewing "rapport." He may start the actual questioning, or turn it over to one of the other members. Frequently, each member undertakes the questioning on a particular area, one in which he is perhaps most competent, so you can expect each member to participate in the examination. Because time is limited, you may also expect some rather abrupt switches in the direction the questioning takes, so do not be upset by it. Normally, a board member will not pursue a single line of questioning unless he discovers a particular strength or weakness.

After each member has participated, the chairman will usually ask whether any member has any further questions, then will ask you if you have anything you wish to add. Unless you are expecting this question, it may floor you. Worse, it may start you off on an extended, extemporaneous speech. The board is not usually seeking more information. The question is principally to offer you a last opportunity to present further qualifications or to indicate that you have nothing to add. So, if you feel that a significant qualification or characteristic has been overlooked, it is proper to point it out in a sentence or so. Do not compliment the board on the thoroughness of their examination – they have been sketchy, and you know it. If you wish, merely say, "No thank you, I have nothing further to add." This is a point where you can "talk yourself out" of a good impression or fail to present an important bit of information. Remember, *you close the interview yourself*.

The chairman will then say, "That is all, Mr. _____, thank you." Do not be startled; the interview is over, and quicker than you think. Thank him, gather your belongings and take your leave. Save your sigh of relief for the other side of the door.

How to put your best foot forward

Throughout this entire process, you may feel that the board individually and collectively is trying to pierce your defenses, seek out your hidden weaknesses and embarrass and confuse you. Actually, this is not true. They are obliged to make an appraisal of your qualifications for the job you are seeking, and they want to see you in your best light. Remember, they must interview all candidates and a non-cooperative candidate may become a failure in spite of their best efforts to bring out his qualifications. Here are 15 suggestions that will help you:

1) Be natural – Keep your attitude confident, not cocky

If you are not confident that you can do the job, do not expect the board to be. Do not apologize for your weaknesses, try to bring out your strong points. The board is interested in a positive, not negative, presentation. Cockiness will antagonize any board member and make him wonder if you are covering up a weakness by a false show of strength.

2) Get comfortable, but don't lounge or sprawl

Sit erectly but not stiffly. A careless posture may lead the board to conclude that you are careless in other things, or at least that you are not impressed by the importance of the occasion. Either conclusion is natural, even if incorrect. Do not fuss with your clothing, a pencil or an ashtray. Your hands may occasionally be useful to emphasize a point; do not let them become a point of distraction.

3) Do not wisecrack or make small talk

This is a serious situation, and your attitude should show that you consider it as such. Further, the time of the board is limited – they do not want to waste it, and neither should you.

4) Do not exaggerate your experience or abilities
In the first place, from information in the application or other interviews and sources, the board may know more about you than you think. Secondly, you probably will not get away with it. An experienced board is rather adept at spotting such a situation, so do not take the chance.

5) If you know a board member, do not make a point of it, yet do not hide it
Certainly you are not fooling him, and probably not the other members of the board. Do not try to take advantage of your acquaintanceship – it will probably do you little good.

6) Do not dominate the interview
Let the board do that. They will give you the clues – do not assume that you have to do all the talking. Realize that the board has a number of questions to ask you, and do not try to take up all the interview time by showing off your extensive knowledge of the answer to the first one.

7) Be attentive
You only have 20 minutes or so, and you should keep your attention at its sharpest throughout. When a member is addressing a problem or question to you, give him your undivided attention. Address your reply principally to him, but do not exclude the other board members.

8) Do not interrupt
A board member may be stating a problem for you to analyze. He will ask you a question when the time comes. Let him state the problem, and wait for the question.

9) Make sure you understand the question
Do not try to answer until you are sure what the question is. If it is not clear, restate it in your own words or ask the board member to clarify it for you. However, do not haggle about minor elements.

10) Reply promptly but not hastily
A common entry on oral board rating sheets is "candidate responded readily," or "candidate hesitated in replies." Respond as promptly and quickly as you can, but do not jump to a hasty, ill-considered answer.

11) Do not be peremptory in your answers
A brief answer is proper – but do not fire your answer back. That is a losing game from your point of view. The board member can probably ask questions much faster than you can answer them.

12) Do not try to create the answer you think the board member wants
He is interested in what kind of mind you have and how it works – not in playing games. Furthermore, he can usually spot this practice and will actually grade you down on it.

13) Do not switch sides in your reply merely to agree with a board member
Frequently, a member will take a contrary position merely to draw you out and to see if you are willing and able to defend your point of view. Do not start a debate, yet do not surrender a good position. If a position is worth taking, it is worth defending.

14) Do not be afraid to admit an error in judgment if you are shown to be wrong

The board knows that you are forced to reply without any opportunity for careful consideration. Your answer may be demonstrably wrong. If so, admit it and get on with the interview.

15) Do not dwell at length on your present job

The opening question may relate to your present assignment. Answer the question but do not go into an extended discussion. You are being examined for a *new* job, not your present one. As a matter of fact, try to phrase ALL your answers in terms of the job for which you are being examined.

Basis of Rating

Probably you will forget most of these "do's" and "don'ts" when you walk into the oral interview room. Even remembering them all will not ensure you a passing grade. Perhaps you did not have the qualifications in the first place. But remembering them will help you to put your best foot forward, without treading on the toes of the board members.

Rumor and popular opinion to the contrary notwithstanding, an oral board wants you to make the best appearance possible. They know you are under pressure – but they also want to see how you respond to it as a guide to what your reaction would be under the pressures of the job you seek. They will be influenced by the degree of poise you display, the personal traits you show and the manner in which you respond.

ABOUT THIS BOOK

This book contains tests divided into Examination Sections. Go through each test, answering every question in the margin. We have also attached a sample answer sheet at the back of the book that can be removed and used. At the end of each test look at the answer key and check your answers. On the ones you got wrong, look at the right answer choice and learn. Do not fill in the answers first. Do not memorize the questions and answers, but understand the answer and principles involved. On your test, the questions will likely be different from the samples. Questions are changed and new ones added. If you understand these past questions you should have success with any changes that arise. Tests may consist of several types of questions. We have additional books on each subject should more study be advisable or necessary for you. Finally, the more you study, the better prepared you will be. This book is intended to be the last thing you study before you walk into the examination room. Prior study of relevant texts is also recommended. NLC publishes some of these in our Fundamental Series. Knowledge and good sense are important factors in passing your exam. Good luck also helps. So now study this Passbook, absorb the material contained within and take that knowledge into the examination. Then do your best to pass that exam.

EXAMINATION SECTION

EXAMINATION SECTION
TEST 1

DIRECTIONS: Each question or incomplete statement is followed by several suggested answers or completions. Select the one that BEST answers the question or completes the statement. PRINT THE LETTER OF THE CORRECT ANSWER IN THE SPACE AT THE RIGHT.

1. When 60,987 is added to 27,835, the result is

    A. 80,712   B. 80,822   C. 87,712   D. 88,822

2. The sum of 693 + 787 + 946 + 355 + 731 is

    A. 3,512   B. 3,502   C. 3,412   D. 3,402

3. When 2,586 is subtracted from 3,003, the result is

    A. 417   B. 527   C. 1,417   D. 1,527

4. When 1.32 is subtracted from 52.6, the result is

    A. 3.94   B. 5.128   C. 39.4   D. 51.28

5. When 56 is multiplied by 438, the result is

    A. 840   B. 4,818   C. 24,528   D. 48,180

6. When 8.7 is multiplied by .34, the result is, most nearly,

    A. 2.9   B. 3.0   C. 29.5   D. 29.6

7. When 1/2 is divided by 2/3, the result is

    A. 1/3   B. 3/4   C. 1 1/3   D. 3

8. When 8,340 is divided by 38, the result is, most nearly

    A. 210   B. 218   C. 219   D. 220

Questions 9-11.

DIRECTIONS: Questions 9 to 11 inclusive are to be answered SOLELY on the basis of the information given below.

Assume that a certain water treatment plant has consumed quantities of chemicals E and F over a five-week period, as indicated in the following table:

Time Period	Number of 100-pound sacks consumed	
	Chemical E	Chemical F
Week 1	5	4
Week 2	7	5
Week 3	6	5
Week 4	8	6
Week 5	6	4

9. The *total* number of pounds of chemical E consumed at the end of the first three weeks is   9.____
   A. 180   B. 320   C. 1,400   D. 1,800

10. According to the table, the week in which the *most* chemicals were consumed was   10.____
    A. week 2   B. week 3   C. week 4   D. week 5

11. According to the table, the *average* number of sacks of chemical F consumed over the first four weeks was   11.____
    A. 4   B. 5   C. 6   D. 7

12. Of the following actions, the *best* one to take FIRST after smoke is seen coming from an electric control device is to   12.____
    A. shut off the power to it
    B. call the main office for advice
    C. look for a wiring diagram
    D. throw water on it

13. Of the following items, the one which would LEAST likely be included on a memorandum is the   13.____
    A. home address of the writer of the memorandum
    B. name of the writer of the memorandum
    C. subject of the memorandum
    D. names or titles of the person who will receive the memorandum

14. When testing joints for leaks in pipe lines containing natural gas, it is BEST to use   14.____
    A. water in the lines under pressure
    B. a lighted candle
    C. an aquastat
    D. soapy water

Questions 15-17.

DIRECTIONS: Questions 15 to 17 inclusive are to be answered SOLELY on the basis of the information given below.

Assume that at various hours of a typical day the amounts of chlorine residual in parts per million (ppm) at a certain water treatment plant are as shown in the following graph:

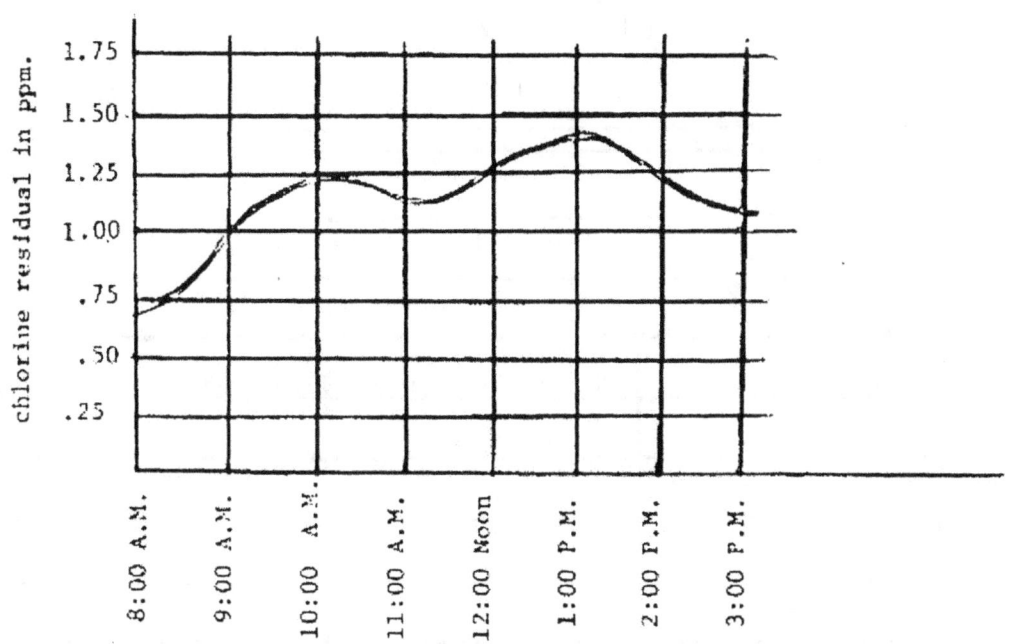

15. According to the graph, the chlorine residual measured in ppm at 9:00 A.M. was, most nearly,

    A. .70   B. .75   C. 1.00   D. 1.25

16. The maximum chlorine residual between 8:00 A.M. and 3:00 P.M. was, most nearly,

    A. .68 ppm   B. 1.10 ppm   C. 1.25 ppm   D. 1.37 ppm

17. According to the graph, between the hour of 12:00 Noon and 1:00 P.M., the chlorine residual was

    A. always increasing
    B. always decreasing
    C. increasing, then decreasing
    D. decreasing, then increasing

18. Of the following statements concerning the use and care of wooden ladders, the *one* which is *TRUE* is that

    A. a light oil should be applied to the rungs to preserve the wood
    B. each rung should be sharply struck with a metal hammer to test its soundness before using it
    C. ladders should be stored in a warm damp area to prevent the wood from getting brittle
    D. tops of ordinary stepladders should not be used as steps

19. It is *poor* practice to use gasoline to clean metal parts that are coated with grease *PRIMARILY* because gasoline

    A. contains lead which is harmful to the user
    B. is a poor solvent for grease
    C. corrodes metal
    D. vapors ignite easily

Questions 20-21.

DIRECTIONS: Questions 20 and 21 are to be answered SOLELY on the basis of the information given in the tables below.

Inventory of 100 pound bags on hand as of 1-1	
Chemical X	16 1/2
Chemical Y	12

Date	Chemical	Number of 100 pound bags used	Number of 100 pound bags received
1-5	X	8 1/2	
1-9	X	3 1/2	
1-9	Y	5	
1-16	X		8
1-18	Y	2 1/2	
1-23	X	3	
1-27	Y	4 1/2	
1-30	X		2
1-31	X	1	

Inventory of 100 pound bags on hand as of 1-31	
Chemical X	
Chemical Y	

J. Doe
Operator

2-2

20. According to the information given in the table, the number of 100-pound bags of chemical Y *on hand* as of 1-31 is

   A. 0   B. 1/2   C. 1   D. 1 1/2

21. According to the information in the table, the *total* number of pounds of chemical X consumed in the month was, most nearly,

   A. 500   B. 1,600   C. 1,800   D. 2,800

Questions 22-27.

DIRECTIONS: Questions 22 to 27 inclusive are to be answered SOLELY on the basis of the paragraph below.

FIRST AID INSTRUCTIONS

The main purpose of first aid is to put the injured person in the best possible position until medical help arrives. This includes the performance of emergency treatment for the purpose of saving a life if a doctor is not present. When a person is hurt, a crowd usually gathers around the victim. If nobody uses his head, the injured person fails to get the care he needs. You must stay calm and, most important, it is your duty to take charge at an accident. The first thing for you to do is to see, as best you can, what is wrong with the injured person. Leave the victim where he is until the nature and extent of his injury are determined. If he is unconscious he should not be moved except to lay him flat on his back if he is in some other position. Loosen the clothing of any seriously hurt person and make him as comfortable as possible. Medical help should be called as soon as possible. You should remain with the injured person and send someone else to call the doctor. You should try to make sure that the one who calls for a doctor is able to give correct information as to the location of the injured person. In order to help the physician to know what equipment may be needed in each particular case, the person making the call should give the doctor as much information about the injury as possible.

22. If nobody uses his head at the scene of an accident, there is danger that

    A. no one will get the names of all the witnesses
    B. a large crowd will gather
    C. the victim will not get the care he needs
    D. the victim will blame the City for negligence

23. When an accident occurs, the FIRST thing you should do is

    A. call a doctor
    B. loosen the clothing of the injured person
    C. notify the victim's family
    D. try to find out what is wrong with the injured person

24. If you do NOT know the extent and nature of the victim's injuries, you should

    A. let the injured person lie where he is
    B. immediately take the victim to a hospital yourself
    C. help the injured person to his feet to see if he can walk
    D. have the injured person sit up on the ground while you examine him

25. If the injured person is breathing and unconscious, you should

    A. get some hot liquid such as coffee or tea in to him
    B. give him artificial respiration
    C. lift up his head to try to stimulate blood circulation
    D. see that he lies flat on his back

26. If it is necessary to call a doctor, you should

    A. go and make the call yourself since you have all the information
    B. find out who the victim's family doctor is before making the call
    C. have someone else make the call who knows the location of the victim
    D. find out which doctor the victim can afford

27. It is important for the caller to give the doctor as much information as is available regarding the injury so that the doctor

    A. can bring the necessary equipment
    B. can make out an accident report
    C. will be responsible for any malpractice resulting from the first aid treatment
    D. can inform his nurse on how long he will be in the field

Questions 28-29.

DIRECTIONS: Questions 28 and 29 are to be answered SOLELY on the basis of the paragraph below.

When a written report must be submitted by an operator to his supervisor, the best rule is "the briefer the better." Obviously, this can be carried to extremes, since all necessary information must be included. However, the ability to write a satisfactory one-page report is an important communication skill. There are several different kinds of reports in common use. One is the form report, which is printed and merely requires the operator to fill in blanks. The greatest problems faced in completion of this report are accuracy and thoroughness. Another type of report is one that must be submitted regularly and systematically. This type of report is known as the periodic report.

28. According to the passage above, accuracy and thoroughness are the GREATEST problems in the completion of

    A. one-page reports   B. form reports
    C. periodic reports   D. long reports

29. According to the passage above, a good written report from an operator to his supervisor should be

    A. printed
    B. formal
    C. periodic
    D. brief

Question 30.

DIRECTIONS: The sketches below show 150-lb. chlorine cylinders stored in three different ways:

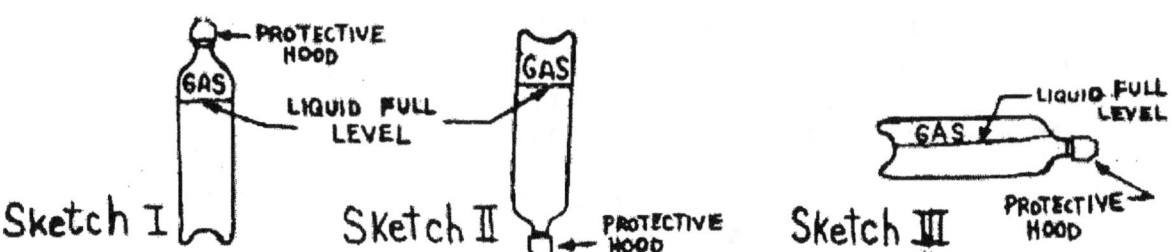

30. *Recommended* practice is to store a 150-lb. chlorine cylinder as shown in

    A. Sketch I *only*
    B. Sketch II *only*
    C. Sketch III *only*
    D. Sketches II and III

31. Of the following, the MOST serious defect in the installation shown below is that

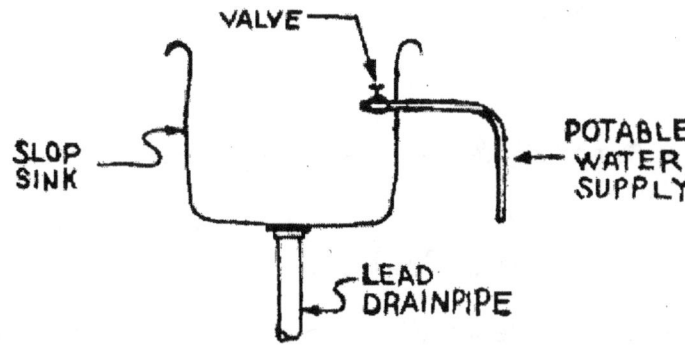

    A. the water supply should be directed downward to prevent excessive splashing over the rim
    B. the above installation may allow backflow of waste water into the water supply line
    C. lead pipes should not be used on drains from fixtures connected to the potable water supply
    D. excessive corrosion will occur on the valve if it becomes submerged

32. Of the following, the distance "x" which would be SAFEST when using the extension ladder shown in the sketch below is

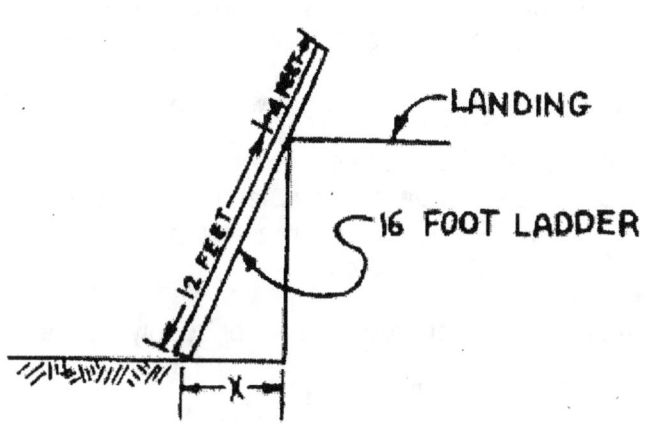

    A. 1 foot   B. 3 feet   C. 5 feet   D. 7 fee

33. Of the following statements regarding safe procedures for lifting a heavy object by yourself from the floor, the one which is FALSE is that

    A. you should keep your back as straight as possible
    B. you should bend your knees
    C. you should mainly use your back muscles in lifting
    D. your feet should be kept clear in case the object is dropped

34. It is generally not considered to be good practice to paint wood ladders. Of the following, the *best* reason for *NOT* painting wood ladders is that

    A. it may hide defects in the wood
    B. the rungs become slippery
    C. the hardware on the ladder becomes unworkable
    D. it would rub off on the surfaces against which it is resting

35. A rip saw would *MOST* likely be used to cut

    A. wood   B. steel   C. copper   D. aluminum

Questions 36-37.

DIRECTIONS: Questions 36 and 37 are to be answered *SOLELY* on the basis of the paragraph below.

NATURAL LAKES

Large lakes may yield water of exceptionally fine quality except near the shore line and in the vicinity of sewer outlets or near outlets of large streams. Therefore, minimum treatment is required. The availability of practically unlimited quantities of water is also a decided advantage. Unfortunately, however, the sewage from a city is often discharged into the same lake from which the water supply is taken. Great care must be taken in locating both the water intake and the sewer outlet so that the pollution handled by the water treatment plant is a minimum.

Sometimes the distance from the shore where dependable, satisfactory water can be found is so great that the cost of water intake facilities is prohibitive for a small municipality. In such cases, another supply must be found, or water must be obtained from a neighboring large city. Lake water is usually uniform in quality from day to day and does not vary in temperature as much as water from a river or small impounding reservoir.

36. A disadvantage of drawing a water supply from a large lake is that

    A. expensive treatment is required
    B. a limited quantity of water is available
    C. nearby cities may dump sewage into the lake
    D. the water is too cold.

37. An advantage of drawing a water supply from a large lake is that the

    A. water is uniform in quality
    B. water varies in temperature
    C. intake is distant from the shore
    D. intake may be near a sewer outlet

38. The *BEST* type of wrench to use to tighten a pipe without marring the pipe surface is   38.____

    A. pipe wrench
    B. strap wrench
    C. spanner wrench
    D. box wrench

39. Of the following statements concerning the use and care of files, the *one* which is *FALSE*   39.____
    is that

    A. files should have tight-fitting handles
    B. rasps are generally used on wood
    C. files should be protected by a light coating of oil when cutting metal
    D. files should be given a quick blow on a wood block to unclog teeth

40. A device which permits flow of a fluid in a pipe in one direction only is known as   40.____

    A. diode
    B. curb box
    C. gooseneck
    D. check valve

KEY (CORRECT ANSWERS)

1.	D	11.	B	21.	B	31.	B
2.	A	12.	A	22.	C	32.	B
3.	A	13.	A	23.	D	33.	C
4.	D	14.	D	24.	A	34.	A
5.	C	15.	C	25.	D	35.	A
6.	B	16.	D	26.	C	36.	C
7.	B	17.	A	27.	A	37.	A
8.	C	18.	D	28.	B	38.	B
9.	D	19.	D	29.	D	39.	C
10.	C	20.	A	30.	A	40.	D

TEST 2

DIRECTIONS: Each question or incomplete statement is followed by several suggested answers or completions. Select the one that *BEST* answers the question or completes the statement. *PRINT THE LETTER OF THE CORRECT ANSWER IN THE SPACE AT THE RIGHT.*

Questions 1-2.

DIRECTIONS: Questions 1 and 2 are to be answered *SOLELY* on the basis of the paragraph below.

PRECIPITATION AND RUNOFF

In the United States, the average annual precipitation is about 30 inches, of which about 21 inches is lost to the atmosphere by evaporation and transpiration. The remaining 9 inches becomes runoff into rivers and lakes. Both the precipitation and runoff vary greatly with geography and season. Annual precipitation varies from more than 100 inches in parts of the northwest to only 2 or 3 inches in parts of the southwest. In the northeastern part of the country, including New York State, the annual average precipitation is about 45 inches, of which about 22 inches becomes runoff. Even in New York State, there is some variation from place to place and considerable variation from time to time. During extremely dry years, the precipitation may be as low as 30 inches and the runoff below 10 inches. In general, there are greater variations in runoff rates from smaller watersheds. A critical water supply situation occurs when there are three or four abnormally dry years in succession.

Precipitation over the state is measured and recorded by a net-work of stations operated by the U. S. Weather Bureau. All of the precipitation records and other data such as temperature, humidity and evaporation rates are published monthly by the Weather Bureau in "Climatological Data." Runoff rates at more than 200 stream-gauging stations in the state are measured and recorded by the U. S. Geological Survey in cooperation with various state agencies. Records of the daily average flows are published annually by the U. S. Geological Survey in "Surface Water Records of New York." Copies may be obtained by writing to the Water Resources Division, United States Geological Survey, Albany, New York 23301.

1. From the above paragraphs it is *appropriate* to conclude that

   A. critical supply situations do not occur
   B. the greater the rainfall, the greater the runoff
   C. there are greater variations in runoff from larger watersheds
   D. the rainfall in the southwest is greater than the average in the country

1.____

2. From the above paragraphs, it is appropriate to conclude that

   A. an annual rainfall of about 50 inches does not occur in New York State
   B. the U. S. Weather Bureau is only interested in rainfall
   C. runoff is equal to rainfall less losses to the atmosphere
   D. information about rainfall and runoff in New York State is unavailable to the public

2.____

3. The following are diagrams of various types of bolt heads. 3.____

   A B C D

   The *one* of the above which is a Phillips head type is the one labelled
   A. A B. B C. C D. D

4. The appearance of frost on the outer surface of a chlorine cylinder which has been 4.____
   placed in service would *MOST* likely indicate that

   A. the cylinder is empty
   B. the gas is escaping too quickly from the cylinder
   C. there is too much pressure in the cylinder
   D. the humidity of the storage area is too high

5. One of the outer belts of a matched set of three V-belts becomes badly frayed. Of the fol- 5.____
   lowing, the *BEST* course of action to take is to

   A. replace only the worn belt
   B. replace only the worn belt but put the new belt in the middle
   C. remove the worn belt, put the center belt on the end and continue running the machine
   D. replace the whole set of belts even if the other two belts show no signs of wear\

6. Of the following, the *BEST* type of valve to use for throttling or when the valve must be 6.____
   opened and closed frequently is a

   A. check valve B. globe valve
   C. butterfly valve D. pop valve

7. Of the following, the device which is used to measure *both* pressure and vacuum is the 7.____

   A. compound gage B. aquastat
   C. pyrometer D. thermocouple

8. Electrical energy is consumed and paid for in units of 8.____

   A. voltage B. ampere-hours
   C. kilowatt-hours D. watts

9. A "governor" on an engine is used to control the engine's 9.____

   A. speed B. temperature
   C. interval of operation
   D. engaging and disengaging the "load"

10. Pressure *below* that of the atmospheric pressure is usually expressed in 10.____

    A. vacuum inches of mercury B. inches of pressure absolute
    C. BTU's D. gallons per minute

11. A short piece of pipe with outside threads at both ends is called a

    A. union B. nipple C. tee D. sleeve

12. Of the following, which device would MOST likely produce water hammer in a plumbing installation? A(n)

    A. relief valve
    B. air chamber
    C. surge tank
    D. quick-closing valve

13. Some portable electric tools have a third conductor in the line cord which is electrically connected to the receptacle box. The reason for this is to

    A. have a spare wire in case one power wire breaks
    B. protect the user of the tool from electrical shock
    C. strengthen the power lead so that it cannot be easily damaged
    D. allow use of the tool for extended periods of time without overheating

14. Of the following, the device which is usually used to measure the rate of flow of water in a pipe is a

    A. pressure gage
    B. Bourden gage
    C. manometer
    D. velocity meter

15. Acid, rosin fluid, or paste applied to metal surfaces to remove oxide film in preparation for soldering is known as

    A. grout B. lampblack C. plumber's soil D. flux

16. In plumbing work, a coil spring which is inserted into a drain to facilitate cleaning of the drain is known as a

    A. pipe reamer B. snake C. plunger D. spigot

17. Of the following, a pneumatic device is one that is driven or powered by

    A. air pressure
    B. oil pressure
    C. water pressure
    D. steam pressure

18. Of the following metals, the one which would MOST likely be used for an electric motor shaft is

    A. wrought iron
    B. hard bronze
    C. steel
    D. bras

19. Of the following, a rotary gear pump is BEST suited for pumping

    A. #6 fuel oil B. hot water C. sewage D. kerosene

20. The MAIN reason for using a flexible coupling to join the shafts of two pieces of machinery together is that a flexible coupling

    A. allows for slight misalignment of the two shafts
    B. can be immediately disengaged in an emergency
    C. will automatically slip when overloaded thus protecting the driver machinery
    D. allows the driven load shaft to continue rotating under its own momentum, when the driver shaft is stopped

21. Of the following, the MAIN purpose of a house trap is to

    A. provide the house drain with a cleanout
    B. prevent gases from the public sewer from entering the house plumbing system
    C. trap articles of value that are accidentally dropped into the drainage pipes
    D. eliminate the necessity for traps under all other plumbing fixtures

22. Of the following, the MAIN reason for sometimes applying bituminous coating to the interiors of steel and cast-iron pipe is that this coating

    A. increases the tensile strength of the pipe
    B. increases the shock resistance of the pipe
    C. removes any objectionable taste from the water imparted by the pipe walls
    D. protects the pipe walls from corrosion

23. The one of the following electrical devices which is most likely to be used to raise or lower A.C. voltages is a

    A. resistor   B. thermistor   C. transformer   D. circuit-breaker

24. When a metal is galvanized, it is given a coating of

    A. nickel   B. tin   C. oxide   D. zinc

25. A conduit hickey is used to

    A. measure conduit pipe   B. bend conduit pipe
    C. thread conduit pipe   D. cut conduit pipe

Questions 26-27.

DIRECTIONS: Questions 26 and 27 are to be answered SOLELY on the basis of the electrical circuit shown below.

26. The circuit above is commonly known as a

    A. series circuit   B. parallel circuit
    C. short circuit   D. circuit breaker

27. The current flowing in the circuit above is

    A. 1 amp   B. 2 amps   C. 3 amps   D. 6 amps

Questions 28-30.

DIRECTIONS: Questions 28 to 30 inclusive are to be answered SOLELY on the basis of the sketches shown below.

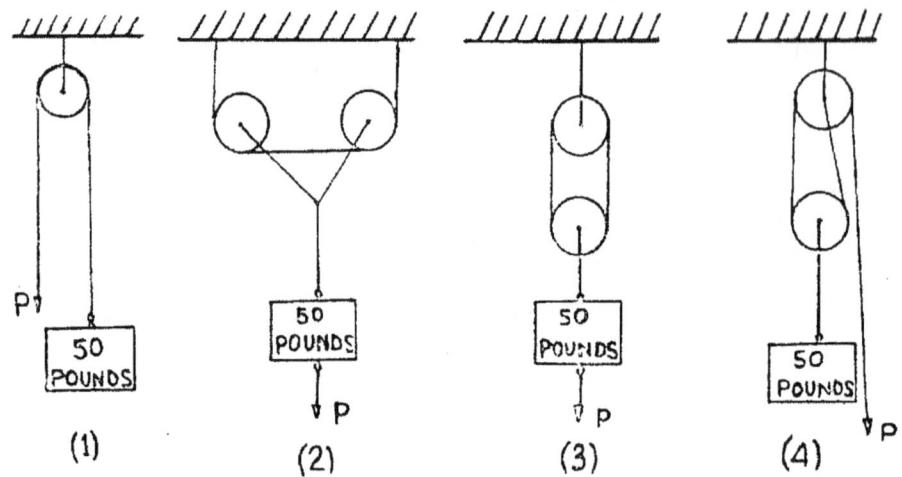

28. The two arrangements in the above diagrams which CANNOT be used to raise the load at all by applying a pull "p" as shown are setups

    A. 1 and 2   B. 2 and 3   C. 3 and 4   D. 1 and 4

29. The arrangement in the diagram above which requires the LEAST effort "p" to move the 50-pound weight is setup

    A. 1   B. 2   C. 3   D. 4

30. The effort required to hold the 50-pound weight at rest off the ground in setup (1) in the diagram above is

    A. 10 pounds   B. 25 pounds   C. 50 pounds   D. 100 pounds

31. Of the following formulas, the one which CORRECTLY shows the relationship between gage pressure and absolute pressure is

    A. Absolute pressure = gage pressure / atmospheric pressure
    B. Absolute pressure + gage pressure = atmospheric pressure
    C. Absolute pressure = gage pressure + atmospheric pressure
    D. Absolute pressure + atmospheric pressure = gage pressure

32. The weight of a gallon of water is, most nearly,

    A. 8.3 pounds   B. 16.6 pounds   C. 24.9 pounds   D. 33.2 pounds

33. Solenoid valves are usually operated

    A. thermally   B. manually   C. hydraulically   D. electrically

34. A 1/2-inch, 8-32 round-head machine screw has

    A. a diameter of 1/2 inch
    B. a length of 8 inches
    C. 8 threads per inch
    D. 32 threads per inch

35. The *MAIN* purpose for the stuffing usually found in centrifugal pump stuffing boxes is

    A. supporting the shaft
    B. controlling the rate of discharge
    C. preventing fluid leakage
    D. compensating for shaft misalignment

36. The *BEST* wrench to use on screwed valves and fittings having hexagonal shape connections is the

    A. chain wrench
    B. open-end wrench
    C. pipe wrench
    D. strap wrench

37. A tap is a tool commonly used to

    A. remove broken screws
    B. flare pipe ends
    C. cut external threads
    D. cut internal threads

38. A thread chaser is *MOST* likely to be used to

    A. rethread damaged threads
    B. remove broken taps
    C. flare tubing
    D. adjust diestocks

39. If an air-conditioning unit shorted out and caught fire, the *BEST* fire extinguisher to use would be a

    A. water extinguisher
    B. foam extinguisher
    C. carbon dioxide extinguisher
    D. soda acid extinguisher

40. Of the following, the *best* action to take to help someone whose eyes have been splashed with lye is to *FIRST*

    A. wash out the eyes with clean water
    B. wash out the eyes with a salt water solution
    C. apply a sterile dressing over the eyes
    D. do nothing to the eyes, but telephone for medical help

---

KEY (CORRECT ANSWERS)

1.	B	11.	B	21.	B	31.	C
2.	C	12.	D	22.	D	32.	A
3.	C	13.	B	23.	C	33.	D
4.	B	14.	D	24.	D	34.	D
5.	D	15.	D	25.	B	35.	C
6.	B	16.	B	26.	A	36.	B
7.	A	17.	A	27.	B	37.	D
8.	C	18.	C	28.	B	38.	A
9.	A	19.	A	29.	D	39.	C
10.	A	20.	A	30.	C	40.	A

EXAMINATION SECTION
TEST 1

DIRECTIONS: Each question or incomplete statement is followed by several suggested answers or completions. Select the one that BEST answers the question or completes the statement. *PRINT THE LETTER OF THE CORRECT ANSWER IN THE SPACE AT THE RIGHT.*

1. A set of round dials MOST likely would be used to

    A. measure the depth of a river
    B. record the volume of water in a well
    C. indicate water pressure
    D. read a gas meter

    1.____

2. A graduated cylinder is MOST likely to be marked in

    A. milligrams
    B. millimeters
    C. centimeters
    D. milliliters

    2.____

Questions 3-4.

DIRECTIONS: Questions 3 and 4 are to be answered on the basis of the following sampling information.

PLANT *Molded Metal Products*
ADDRESS *1003 E. Diversey* STA. *24*
CITY *Chicago* PIPE SIZE *10"*
PHONE # _____ AREA *Central*

SANITARY SEWER
WATERWAY
OTHER
DATE *4/6*

MILITARY TIME	CLARIFY (Clear, Cloudy, Color . Etc.)	FLOW	WEATHER & CONDITIONS	pH	REMARKS
1415	Cloudy, susp., particles	Medium 2"	50s cloudy	9.8	Sample has yellow green tint
1442	Cloudy, susp., particles	High 3"	50s rain	10.0	Sample has yellow tint pH grab
1516	Cloudy, susp., particles	Medium 2"	50s rain	10.0	Sample has yellow green tint
1541	Cloudy, susp., particles	Medium 2"	40s cloudy	1..0	Sample has yellow green tint
1616	Cloudy, susp., particles	High 3"	40s rain	10.0	Sample has yellow tint
1647	Cloudy, susp., particles	Medium 2"	40s cloudy	10	Sample has yellow tint pH grab
1712	Cloudy, susp., particles	High 3"	30s cloudy	10	Sample has yellow green tint
1742	Cloudy, susp., particles	Medium 2"	30s rain	10	Sample has yellow tint pH grab

OBSERVATIONS: Molded Metal Products has taken over business of Miller Metalworks: Miller stored toxic chemicals in in area.
WATER METER READINGS & TIME: 2" Rockwell #1172332 Read #1323 lbs. 01473
GRAB SAMPLES & TIME TAKEN: (1) 1415 LAB # 4329C (2) 1448 LAB #43300
                            (1) 1412 LAB # 4331C (2) 1218 LAB #4332C

3. How many pH measurements were recorded in this report?

   A. None B. Three C. Eight D. Eleven

4. During what period of time were the MOST grab samples taken? Between _____ P.M.

   A. 2 and 3 B. 3 and 4 C. 4 and 5 D. 5 and 6

Questions 5-6.

DIRECTIONS: Questions 5 and 6 are to be answered on the basis of the fuel gauge shown below. The tank holds 23 gallons.

5. How much fuel is in the tank?
   _____ gallons.

   A. 12.5 B. 15.6 C. 13.8 D. 14.4

6. What percentage of the fuel in the tank has been used?
   _____ percent.

   A. 38 B. 40 C. 46 D. 32

Questions 7-8.

DIRECTIONS: Questions 7 and 8 are to be answered on the basis of the following map.

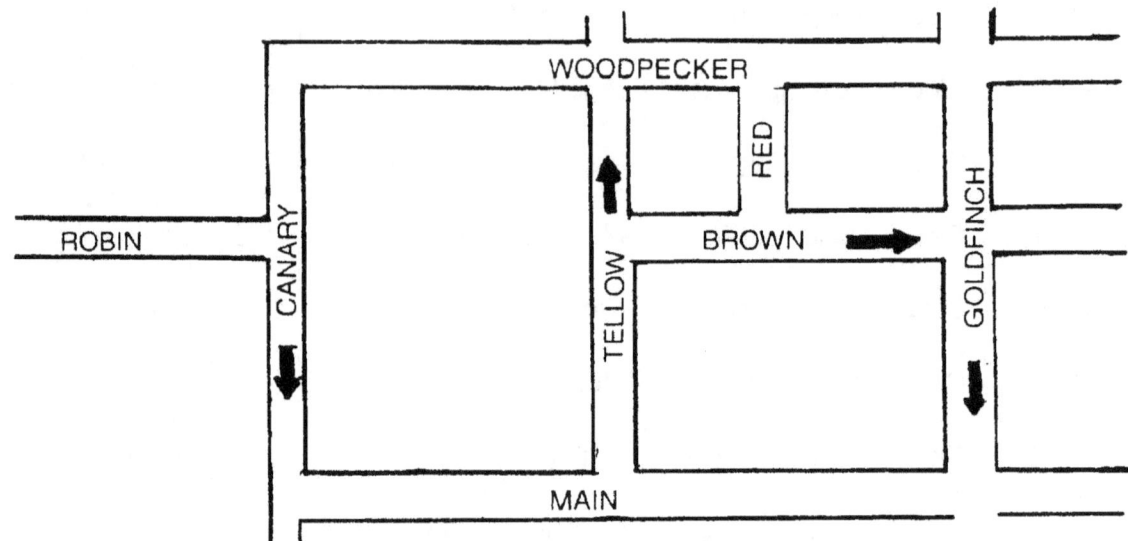

7. From Brown (east of Red) to Robin.

   A. Left on Goldfinch, left on Woodpecker, left on Canary, right on Robin
   B. Right on Goldfinch, right on Main, right on Yellow, left on Woodpecker, left on Canary, right on Robin
   C. Right on Goldfinch, right on Main, right on Canary, left on Robin
   D. Right on Goldfinch, left on Main, right on Canary, right on Robin

8. From Canary to Red.

    A. Left on Main, left on Goldfinch, left on Woodpecker, left on Red
    B. Left on Main, left on Yellow, left on Woodpecker, right on Red
    C. Left on Main, left on Yellow, right on Brown, left on Red
    D. Right on Main, left on Goldfinch, left on Brown, right on Red

8._____

Questions 9-10.

DIRECTIONS: Questions 9 and 10 are to be answered on the basis of the following chart.

PROBLEM/CAUSES	REMEDIES
Sampler distributor does not advance smoothly; liquid missing bottle	
Spout binding or plugged	Disassemble and clean
Improper spout alignment	Realign; check for smooth operation of stepper motor; motor should have 24 positive positions; replace motor if necessary
Electronic malfunction	Isolate and replace bad component
Sampler does not shut down after 24 bottles	
Front panel switch in COMPOSITE position	Place toggle switch in either BOTTLES PER SAMPLE or SAMPLES PER BOTTLE position
Defective stepper motor	Apply 12 volts across leads to test. Replace as necessary.
Electronic malfunction of count circuit	Isolate and replace bad component. Consult factory.
Fuse blowing	
Improper pump motor alignment (5 amp fuse)	Realign for lowest current draw (standard pump - 1.5 amps, FAS-FLO pump 3.5 amps). Check for binding coupling or loose bushing.
Bad motor or motor brushes causing high current draw (5 amp fuse)	Replace brushes; clean commutater; consult factory.
Improper fuse size or type (5 or 1 amp fuse)	Replace fuses with 5 amp and 1 amp *Slo-Blo* type
Improper tubing in pump (5 amp fuse)	Replace pump tubing with medical grade silicone or equivalent (3/8" internal diameter and 1/8" wall)
Improper spacing of pump tubing collars (5 amp fuse)	Reposition collars on pump tubing insert exactly 10 1/4" (26 cm) apart. Measure from center of collar groove.
Bad transformer (1 amp fuse)	Check for shorted connections. Consult factory.

9. Improper pump tubing can cause a 9._____

   A. sampler to blow fuses
   B. distributor to malfunction
   C. defective stepper motor
   D. sampler to overfill bottles

10. What is the MOST likely remedy for improper spout alignment? Checking 10._____

    A. alignment of the pump motor
    B. operation of the stepper motor
    C. the position of the toggle switch
    D. for electronic malfunctions

Questions 11-12.

DIRECTIONS: Questions 11 and 12 are to be answered on the basis of the following chart.

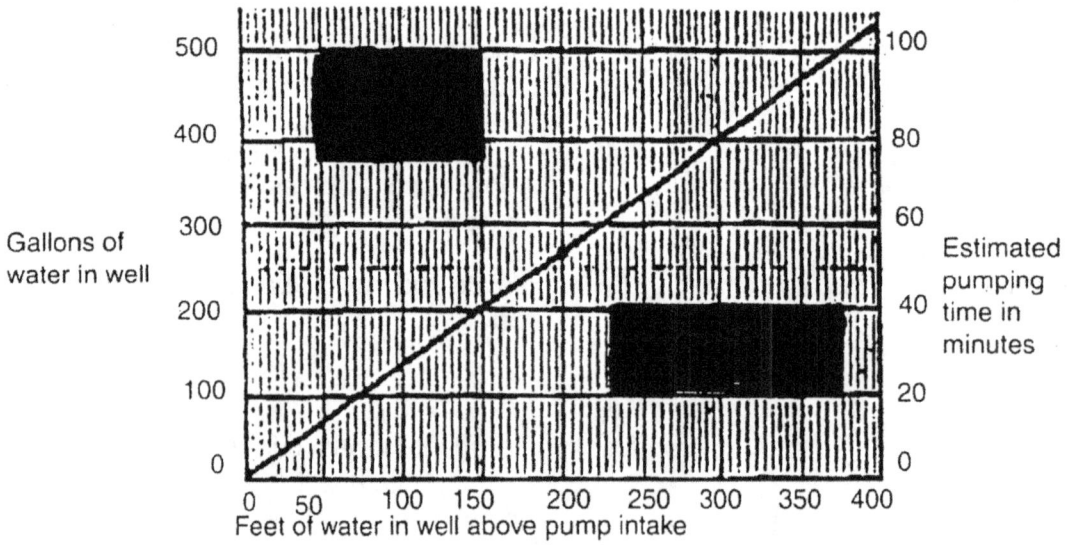

11. How long should it take to empty the well if there is 150 feet of water in the well above the pump intake? _____ minutes. 11._____

    A. 25   B. 30   C. 35   D. 40

12. What is the BEST estimate of the number of gallons in the well when it registers 200 feet above the pump intake? 12._____
    _____ gallons.

    A. 225   B. 240   C. 270   D. 300

Questions 13-14.

DIRECTIONS: Questions 13 and 14 are to be answered on the basis of the following sampling information.

Sample each station every 30 minutes for as long as time permits. Read all 3 water meters daily. Measure pH on-site; grab samples if warranted.

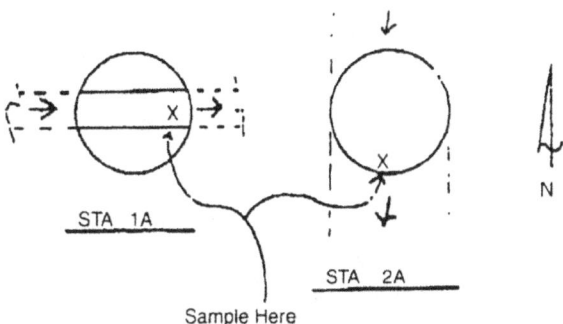

13. What is the direction of flow in Station 2A? From _____ to _____. 13._____

 A. west; east B. east; west
 C. north; south D. south; north

14. How often are samples to be gathered at this site? 14._____

 A. From each station every 30 minutes for as long as possible
 B. From Station 1A every 30 minutes until filling bottles
 C. From Station 2A every 30 minutes as long as flow permits
 D. Twice an hour from each station until bottles are full

Questions 15-16.

DIRECTIONS: Questions 15 and 16 are to be answered on the basis of the following containers.

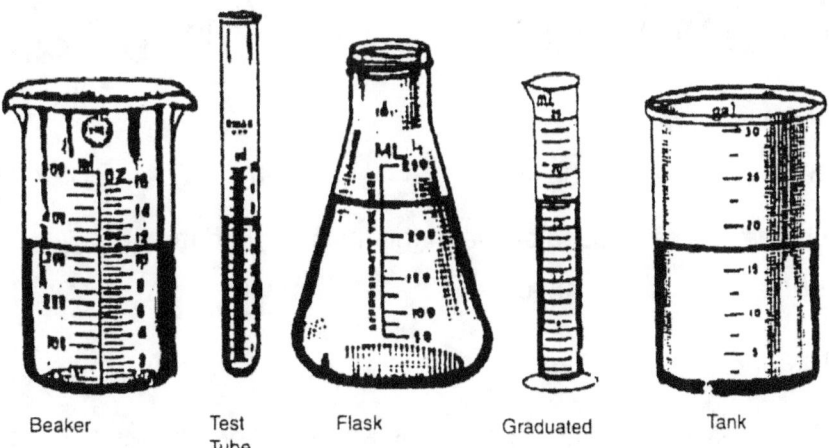

15. How much fluid is in the beaker? 15._____

 A. 225 ml B. 17.5 gal. C. 12.5 oz. D. 325 ml.

16. How much fluid is in the tank?   16.___

    A. 325 ml   B. 12.5 oz.   C. 17.5 gal.   D. 225 ml.

17. Used seals from presealed bottles are to be   17.___

    A. discarded immediately after initial use
    B. saved and turned in at the end of each day
    C. reused on other samples until they wear out
    D. initiated and placed back on original bottles

18. Presealed bottles are used to   18.___

    A. assure that company splits are uncontaminated   18.___
    B. prove in court that samples have not been altered
    C. satisfy city ordinances to store only sealed samples
    D. prevent lawsuits against Sanitary District employees

Questions 19-20.

DIRECTIONS: Questions 19 and 20 are to be answered on the basis of the following meters.

METER I   METER II

METER III   METER IV

19. What does Meter II read?   19.___

    A. 2967   B. 3078   C. 2901   D. 2067

20. How much gas has been used between the first and third meters? _____ cu. ft.   20.___

    A. 4450   B. 4590   C. 2346   D. 2104

Questions 21-22.

DIRECTIONS: Questions 21 and 22 are to be answered on the basis of the following chart.

AVERAGE READINGS AND RANGES

WELL NUMBER	MW-1	MW-2	MW-2
pH Reading	6.7 - 7.2	6.9 - 8.0	7.0 - 8.1
Conductivity Reading (MHOS)	2.0 - 3.6 ($\times 10^3$)	0.85 - 1.30 ($\times 10^3$)	0.80 - 1.1 ($\times 10^3$)
Temperature of Sample (°C) Summer	14 - 15	14 - 15	14 - 15
Winter	11 - 13	11 - 13	11 - 13
First Pump Down	165%	90%	90%
Initial Elevation (Feet)	62	67	87
Initial Volume (Gallons)	455	437	264
Purge Volume (Gallons)	750	413	237
Final Elevation (Feet)	69	134	127

21. Which statement is MOST accurate based on the above report?

    A. The lowest pH readings will always be from well MW-2.
    B. Samples in all three wells are always the same temperature.
    C. The largest purge volume is in well MW-1.
    D. A pH reading of 7.5 would be considered high in well MW-3.

22. Which statement is MOST accurate based on the above report?

    A. The average initial elevation in the three wells is 72 feet.
    B. The initial elevation in well MW-2 is 134 feet.
    C. The average final elevation in the three wells is 330 feet.
    D. Each well can hold at least 350 gallons.

23. What are the MOST appropriate steps in responding to evidence of hazardous fumes in the area?

    A. Attend injured personnel; call for help; evacuate the area
    B. Evacuate; maintain ventilation; assist injured personnel
    C. Call for help; attend injured personnel; evacuate the area
    D. Maintain ventilation; evacuate; call for help

24. The hazards of H_2S include all of the following EXCEPT it is

    A. water soluble
    B. corrosive to many metals
    C. colorless and odorless
    D. absorbed through the skin

25. Toxic chemicals discharged into water have been found to be

    A. potable
    B. pathogens
    C. carcinogens
    D. radioactive

KEY (CORRECT ANSWERS)

1.	D	11.	D
2.	D	12.	C
3.	C	13.	C
4.	A	14.	A
5.	D	15.	D
6.	A	16.	C
7.	B	17.	B
8.	C	18.	B
9.	A	19.	A
10.	B	20.	D

21. C
22. A
23. B
24. D
25. C

EXAMINATION SECTION
TEST 1

DIRECTIONS: Each question or incomplete statement is followed by several suggested answers or completions. Select the one that BEST answers the question or completes the statement. *PRINT THE LETTER OF THE CORRECT ANSWER IN THE SPACE AT THE RIGHT.*

Questions 1-17.

DIRECTIONS: Questions 1 through 17 are to be answered on the basis of the tools shown below and on the following page. The numbers in the answers refer to the numbers beneath the tools.

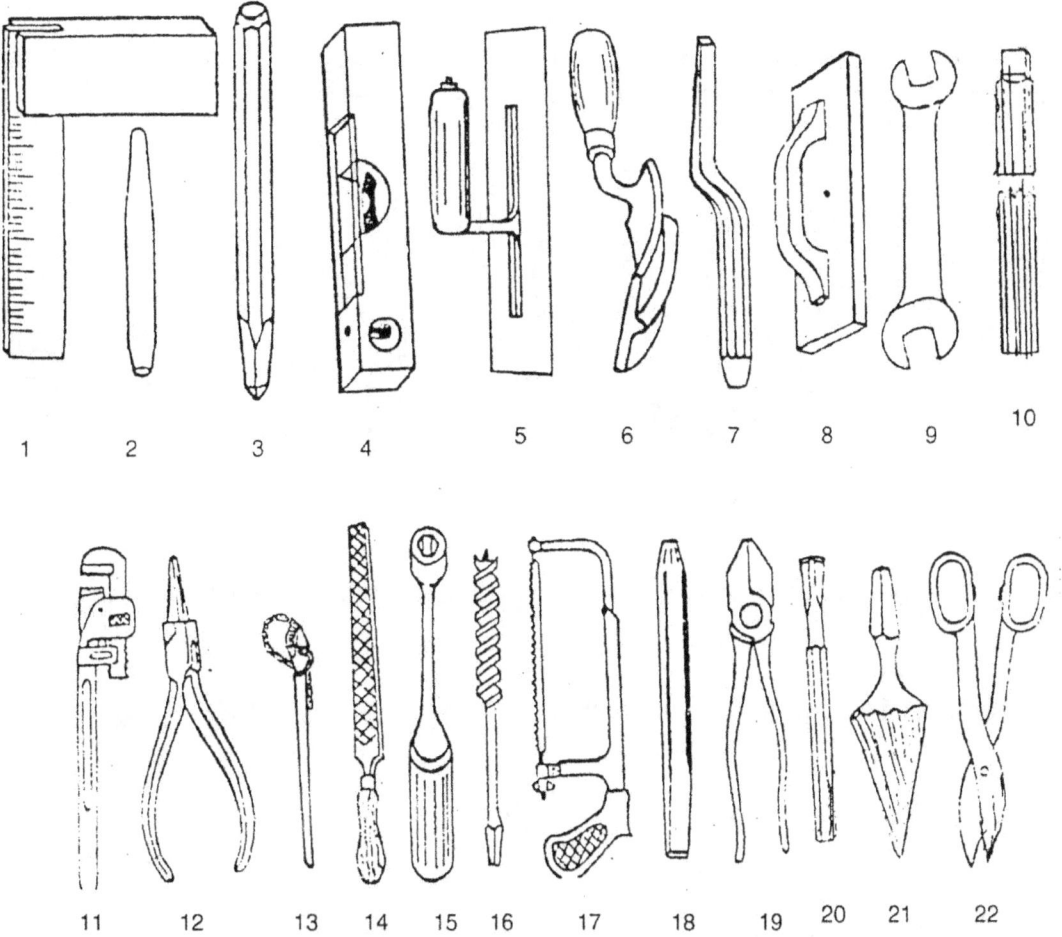

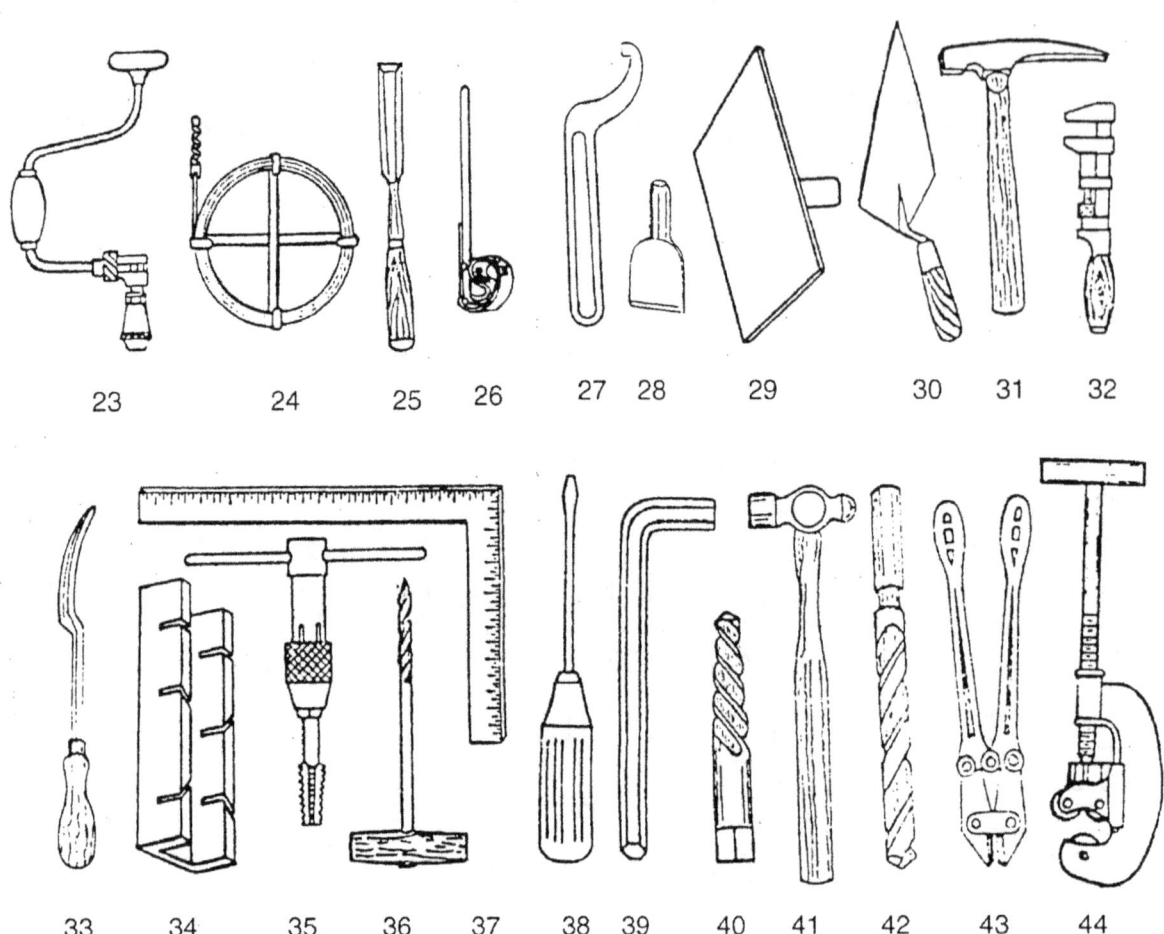

1. To tighten an elbow onto a threaded pipe, a mechanic should use tool number
   A. 9   B. 11   C. 26   D. 32

2. To cut grooves in newly poured cement, a mechanic should use tool number
   A. 5   B. 6   C. 28   D. 29

3. To *caulk* a lead joint, a mechanic should use tool number
   A. 7   B. 10   C. 25   D. 33

4. The term *snips* should be applied by a mechanic to tool number
   A. 12   B. 22   C. 36   D. 43

5. To slightly enlarge an existing 17/32" diameter hole in a metal plate, a mechanic should use tool number
   A. 3   B. 10   C. 14   D. 35

6. The term *snake* should be applied by a mechanic to tool number
   A. 21   B. 23   C. 24   D. 40

7. If the threaded portion of a 1/2" brass pipe breaks off inside a gate valve, the piece should be removed with tool number   7._____

    A. 15   B. 35   C. 39   D. 40

8. To cut a face brick into a bat, a mechanic should use tool number   8._____

    A. 3   B. 18   C. 25   D. 28

9. A mechanic should cut a 3" x 2" x 3/16" angle iron with tool number   9._____

    A. 3   B. 17   C. 22   D. 43

10. A mechanic should tighten a chrome-plated water supply pipe by using tool number   10._____

    A. 11   B. 19   C. 26   D. 32

11. The term *hawk* should be applied by a mechanic to tool number   11._____

    A. 28   B. 29   C. 30   D. 33

12. If your co-worker asks you to pass him the *star* drill, you should hand him tool number   12._____

    A. 16   B. 20   C. 40   D. 42

13. After threading a 1" diameter piece of pipe, a mechanic should debur the inside by using tool number   13._____

    A. 14   B. 21   C. 36   D. 40

14. A mechanic should apply the term *float* to tool number   14._____

    A. 4   B. 6   C. 8   D. 28

15. If a mechanic has to cut a dozen 15-inch lengths of 3/4-inch steel pipe for spacers, he should use tool number   15._____

    A. 18   B. 26   C. 43   D. 44

16. If a mechanic is erecting two structural steel plates and needs to line up the bolt holes, he should use tool number   16._____

    A. 2   B. 3   C. 33   D. 42

17. To cut reinforcing wire mesh to be used in a concrete floor, you should use tool number   17._____

    A. 7   B. 17   C. 18   D. 43

18. The MAIN reason for overhauling a power tool on a regular basis is to   18._____

    A. make the men more familiar with the tool
    B. keep the men busy during slack times
    C. insure that the tool is used occasionally
    D. minimize breakdowns

19. A mechanic should NOT press too heavily on a hacksaw while using it to cut through a steel rod because this may   19._____

    A. create flying steel particles   B. bend the frame
    C. break the blade   D. overheat the rod

20. Creosote is commonly used with wood to

    A. speed-up the seasoning
    B. make the wood fireproof
    C. make painting easier
    D. preserve the wood

21. A mitre box should be used to

    A. hold a saw while sharpening it
    B. store expensive tools
    C. hold a saw at a fixed angle
    D. encase steel beams for protection

22. Wood scaffold planks should be inspected

    A. at regular intervals
    B. before they are stored away
    C. once a week
    D. each time before they are used

23. Continuous sheeting should be used when excavating deep trenches in

    A. rock
    B. stiff clay
    C. firm earth
    D. unstable soil

24. The MAIN reason for requiring that certain special tools be returned to the tool room after a job has been completed is that

    A. missing tools can be replaced
    B. the men will not need to care for the tools
    C. more tools will be available for use
    D. this permits easier inspection and maintenance of tools

25. The BEST material to use to extinguish an oil fire is

    A. sand
    B. water
    C. sawdust
    D. stone gravel

26. A *lally* column is

    A. fabricated from angles and plates
    B. fabricated by tying two channels together with lattice bars
    C. a steel member that has unequal sections
    D. a pipe fitted with a base plate at each end

27. The BEST action for you to take if you discover a small puddle of oil on the shop floor is to FIRST

    A. have it cleaned up
    B. find out who spilled it
    C. discover the source of the leak
    D. cover it with newspaper

28. You should listen to your foreman even when he insists on explaining the procedure for a job you have done many times before because

    A. you can do the job the way you want when he leaves
    B. he may make an error and you can show that you know your job
    C. it is wise to humor him even if he is wrong
    D. you are required to do the job the way the foreman wants it

28._____

Questions 29-34.

DIRECTIONS: Questions 29 through 34 refer to the sketches shown to the right of each question.

29. The indicated pressure is MOST NEARLY _____ psi.
    A. 132
    B. 137
    C. 143
    D. 148

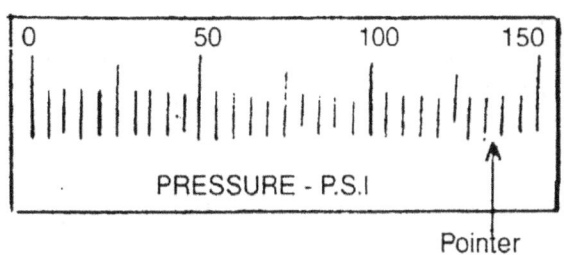

29._____

30. The fewest number of shims, of any combination of thicknesses, required to exactly fill the 1/4" gap shown is
    A. 7
    B. 8
    C. 9
    D. 10

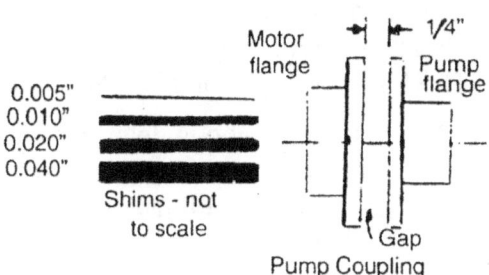

30._____

31. The dimension X on the keyway shown is
    A. 3 3/8"
    B. 3 9/16"
    C. 3 3/4"
    D. 4"

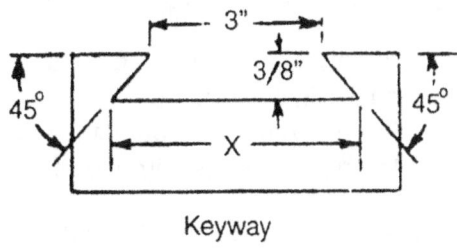

Keyway

31._____

32. If the tank gage reads 120 psi, then the pipe gage should read _____ psi.
    A. 80
    B. 120
    C. 180
    D. 240

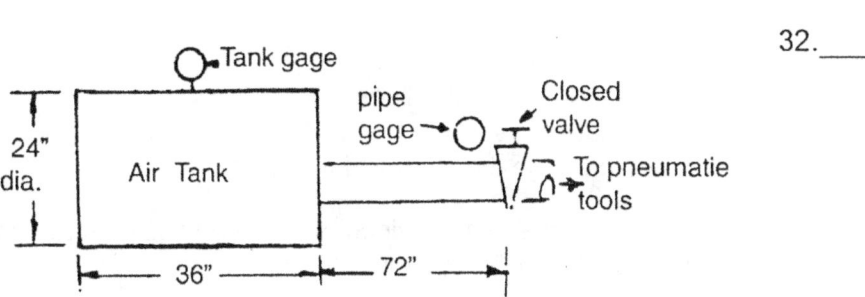

32._____

33. The MINIMUM number of feet of chainlink fence needed to completely enclose the storage yard shown is
    A. 278
    B. 286
    C. 295
    D. 304

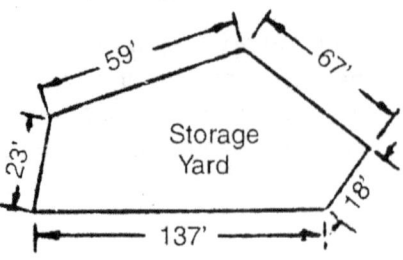

34. The distance X between the holes is
    A. 1 7/8"
    B. 2 1/16"
    C. 2 3/8"
    D. 2 9/16"

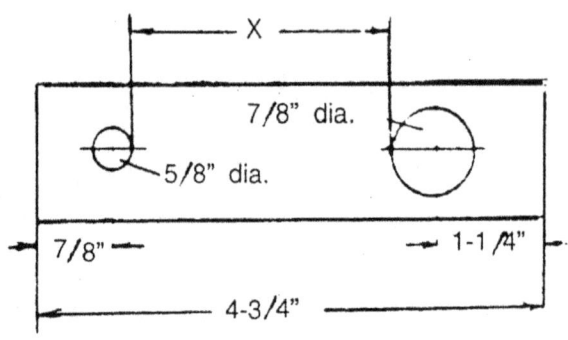

35. A rule of the Transit Authority is that all employees are required to report defective equipment to their superiors, even when the maintenance of the particular equipment is handled by someone else.
The MAIN purpose of this rule is to
    A. determine who is doing his job improperly
    B. have repairs made before trouble occurs
    C. encourage all employees to be alert at all times
    D. reduce the cost of equipment

36. Some equipment is fitted with wing nuts.
Such nuts are especially useful when
    A. the nut is to be wired closed
    B. space is limited
    C. the equipment is subject to vibration
    D. the nuts must be removed frequently

37. It is considered bad practice to use water to put out electrical fires MAINLY because the water may
    A. rust the equipment
    B. short circuit the lines
    C. cause a serious shock
    D. damage the electrical insulation

38. While you are being trained, you will be assigned to work with an experienced mechanic.
It would be BEST for you to
    A. remind the mechanic that he is responsible for your training
    B. tell him frequently how much you know about the work
    C. let him do all the work while you observe closely
    D. be as cooperative and helpful as you can

39. The BEST instrument to use to make certain that two points, separated by a vertical distance of 9 feet, are in perfect vertical alignment is a

    A. square   B. level   C. plumb bob   D. protractor

40. If a measurement scaled from a drawing is one inch, and the scale of the drawing is 1/8-inch to the foot, then the one inch measurement would represent an actual length of

    A. 8 feet
    C. 1/8 of a foot
    B. 2 feet
    D. 8 inches

KEY (CORRECT ANSWERS)

1.	B	11.	B	21.	C	31.	C
2.	B	12.	B	22.	D	32.	B
3.	A	13.	B	23.	D	33.	D
4.	B	14.	C	24.	D	34.	A
5.	B	15.	D	25.	A	35.	B
6.	C	16.	A	26.	D	36.	D
7.	D	17.	D	27.	A	37.	C
8.	D	18.	D	28.	D	38.	D
9.	B	19.	C	29.	B	39.	C
10.	C	20.	D	30.	A	40.	A

TEST 2

DIRECTIONS: Each question or incomplete statement is followed by several suggested answers or completions. Select the one that BEST answers the question or completes the statement. *PRINT THE LETTER OF THE CORRECT ANSWER IN THE SPACE AT THE RIGHT.*

1. Cloth tapes should NOT be used when accurate measurements must be obtained because 1.____

    A. the numbers soon become worn and thus difficult to read
    B. there are not enough subdivisions of each inch on the tape
    C. the ink runs when wet, thus making the tape difficult to read
    D. small changes in the pull on the tape will make considerable differences in tape readings

2. It is considered good practice to release the pressure from an air hose before uncoupling the hose connection because this avoids 2.____

    A. wasting air
    B. possible personal injury
    C. damage to the air tool
    D. damage to the air compressor

3. In brick construction, a structural steel member is used to support the wall above door and window openings. This member is called a 3.____

    A. purlin   B. sill   C. truss   D. lintel

Questions 4-9.

DIRECTIONS: Questions 4 through 9 show the top view of an object in the first column, the front view of the same object in the second column and four drawings in the third column, one of which correctly represents the RIGHT side view of the object. Select the CORRECT right side view. As a guide, the first one is an illustrative example, the CORRECT answer of which is C.

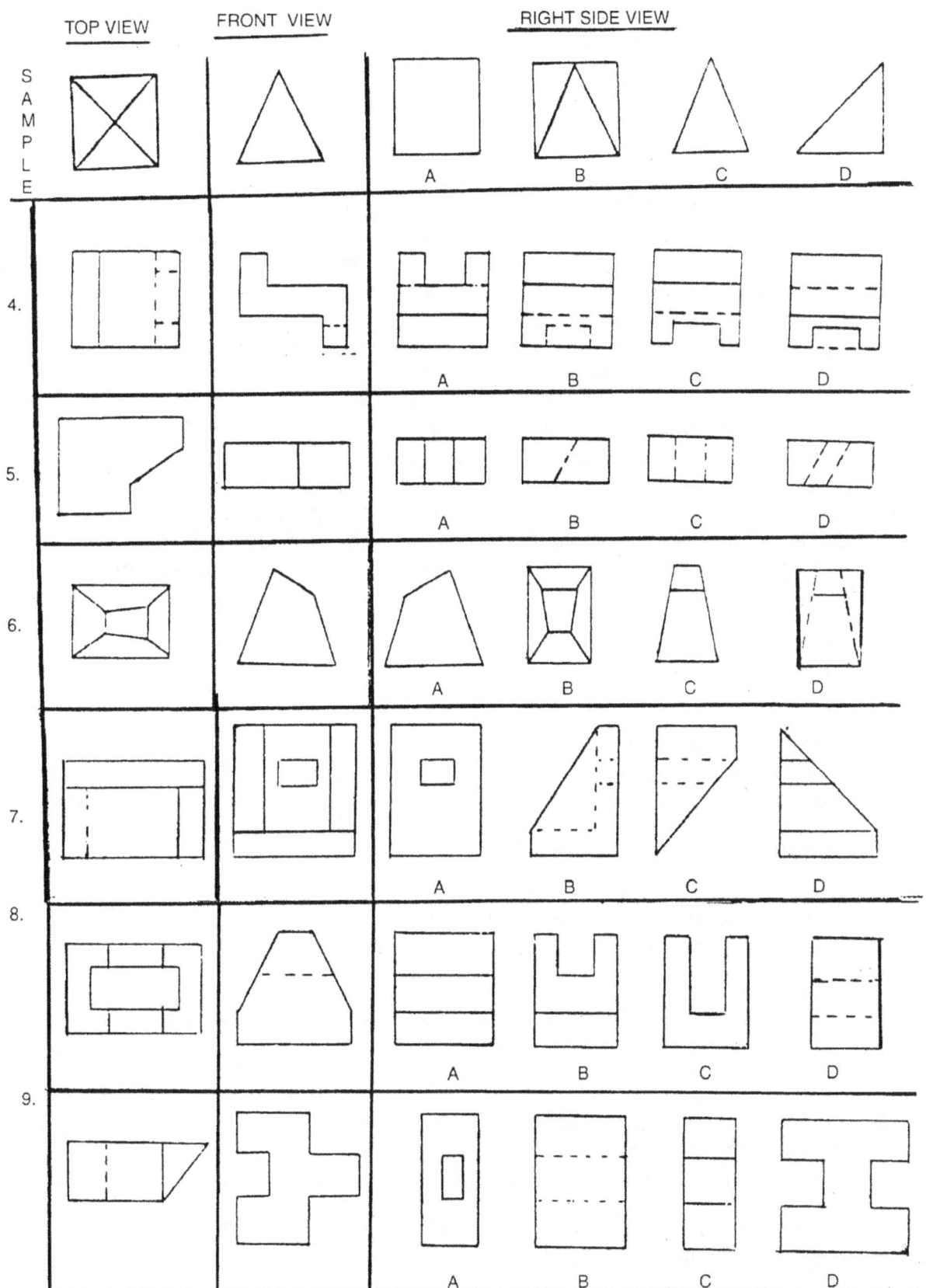

Questions 10-14.

DIRECTIONS: Questions 10 through 14 are to be answered on the basis of the information contained in the safety regulations given below. In answering these questions, refer to these rules.

REGULATIONS FOR SMALL GROUPS WHO MOVE FROM POINT TO POINT ON THE TRACKS

Employees who perform duties on the tracks in small groups and who move from point to point along the trainway must be on the alert at all times and prepared to clear the track when a train approaches without unnecessarily slowing it down. Underground at all times, and out-of-doors between sunset and sunrise, such employees must not enter upon the tracks unless each of them is equipped with an approved light. Flashlights must not be used for protection by such groups. Upon clearing the track to permit a train to pass, each member of the group must give a proceed signal, by hand or light, to the motorman of the train. Whenever such small groups are working in an area protected by caution lights or flags, but are not members of the gang for whom the flagging protection was established, they must not give proceed signals to motormen. The purpose of this rule is to avoid a motorman's confusing such signal with that of the flagman who is protecting a gang. Whenever a small group is engaged in work of an engrossing nature or at any time when the view of approaching trains is limited by reason of curves or otherwise, one man of the group, equipped with a whistle, must be assigned properly to warn and protect the man or men at work and must not perform any other duties while so assigned.

10. If a small group of men are traveling along the tracks toward their work location and a train approaches, they should

    A. stop the train
    B. signal the motorman to go slowly
    C. clear the track
    D. stop immediately

10._____

11. Small groups may enter upon the tracks

    A. only between sunset and sunrise
    B. provided each has an approved light
    C. provided their foreman has a good flashlight
    D. provided each man has an approved flashlight

11._____

12. After a small group has cleared the tracks in an area unprotected by caution lights or flags,

    A. each member must give the proceed signal to the motorman
    B. the foreman signals the motorman to proceed
    C. the motorman can proceed provided he goes slowly
    D. the last member off the tracks gives the signal to the motorman

12._____

13. If a small group is working in an area protected by the signals of a track gang, the members of the small group

    A. need not be concerned with train movement
    B. must give the proceed signal together with the track gang

13._____

C. can delegate one of their members to give the proceed signal
D. must not give the proceed signal

14. If the view of approaching trains is blocked, the small group should 14._____

    A. move to where they can see the trains
    B. delegate one of the group to warn and protect them
    C. keep their ears alert for approaching trains
    D. refuse to work at such locations

15. The information in an accident report which may be MOST useful in helping to prevent similar-type accidents from happening is the 15._____

    A. cause of the accident
    B. time of day it happened
    C. type of injuries suffered
    D. number of people injured

16. The MAIN reason why each coat of paint should be of a different color when two coats of paint are specified is that 16._____

    A. cheaper paint can be used as the undercoat
    B. less care need be taken in applying the coats
    C. any missed areas will be easier to spot
    D. the colors do not have to be exact

Questions 17-23.

DIRECTIONS: Questions 17 through 23 refer to the sketches shown to the right of each question.

17. The distance y is 17._____
    A. 5/8"
    B. 7/8"
    C. 1 1/8"
    D. 1 3/8"

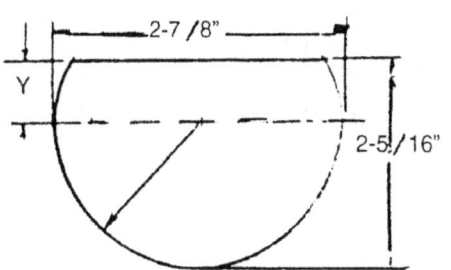

18. The sketch shows the float-operated trippers for operating a sump pump. If you want the pump to start sooner, you should _____ tripper. 18._____
    A. *lower* the upper
    B. *lower* the lower
    C. *raise* the upper
    D. *raise* the lower

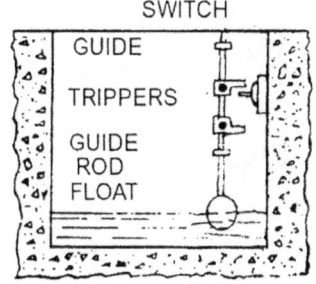

19. The width of the wood stud shown is
    A. 1 1/8"
    B. 1 5/16"
    C. 1 5/8"
    D. 3 5/8"

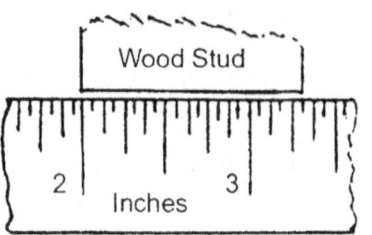

19.____

20. The right angle shown has been divided into four unequal parts.
    The number of degrees in angle X is
    A. 31°
    B. 33°
    C. 38°
    D. 45°

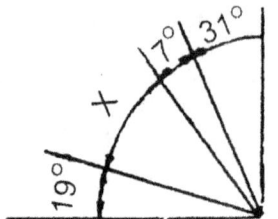

20.____

21. The reading on the meter shown is MOST NEARLY
    A. 0465
    B. 0475
    C. 0566
    D. 1566

21.____

22. The length X of the slot shown is
    A. 2 3/8"
    B. 2 7/16"
    C. 2 1/2"
    D. 2 9/16"

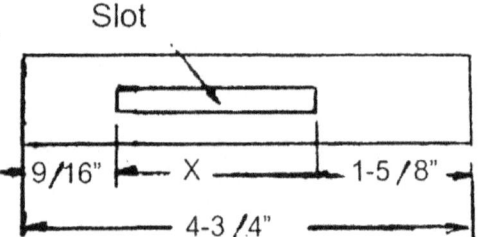

22.____

23. The volume of the bar shown is _____ cubic inches.
    A. 132
    B. 356
    C. 420
    D. 516

23.____

24. Gaskets should be used with

    A. flanged pipe fittings B. bell and spigot pipe
    C. threaded reducing couplings D. threaded bushings

24.____

25. The MAIN purpose for providing a plumbing fixture with a trap is to

    A. equalize the pressures in the drainage system
    B. catch any article that might plug the drain
    C. prevent passage of gases
    D. supply an easy means of cleaning if the fixture gets plugged

26. The *soil stack* of a drainage system is left open at its upper end in order to

    A. prevent the sewer from backing up into the traps
    B. prevent the siphoning of traps
    C. prevent ventilation of the drainage system
    D. hold a vacuum above the house drain line

27. Under the city color coding of pipes, drinking water pipes should be painted

    A. blue   B. yellow   C. green   D. red

28. When changing from a 2" pipe size to a 1" pipe in a horizontal steam line, the PROPER fitting to be used is a(n)

    A. concentric bushing   B. face bushing
    C. concentric reducer   D. eccentric reducer

29. An expansion slip joint

    A. permits longitudinal movement of a pipe
    B. is used when the pipe has been cut short
    C. compensates for differences in pipe pressure
    D. permits small movement for lining pipe hangers

30. The MAIN reason why brass is better than iron for water piping is that brass is

    A. cheaper   B. lighter
    C. stronger   D. more corrosion resistant

31. A bell and spigot cast iron pipe joint is made water-tight by

    A. rolling and beading the ends
    B. caulking with oakum and lead
    C. caulking with cotton wick and cement
    D. applying sealing compound to the threaded ends

32. The one of the following valves which is ALWAYS automatic in operation is the _____ valve.

    A. gate   B. angle   C. check   D. globe

33. Threaded joints may be made up tight by using pipe thread compound. The CORRECT procedure is to apply the compound

    A. only to the male threads
    B. only to the female threads
    C. to both male and female threads
    D. to either the male or female thread, depending on the pipe size

Questions 34-39.

DIRECTIONS: Questions 34 through 39 are to be answered on the basis of the riser diagram shown below.

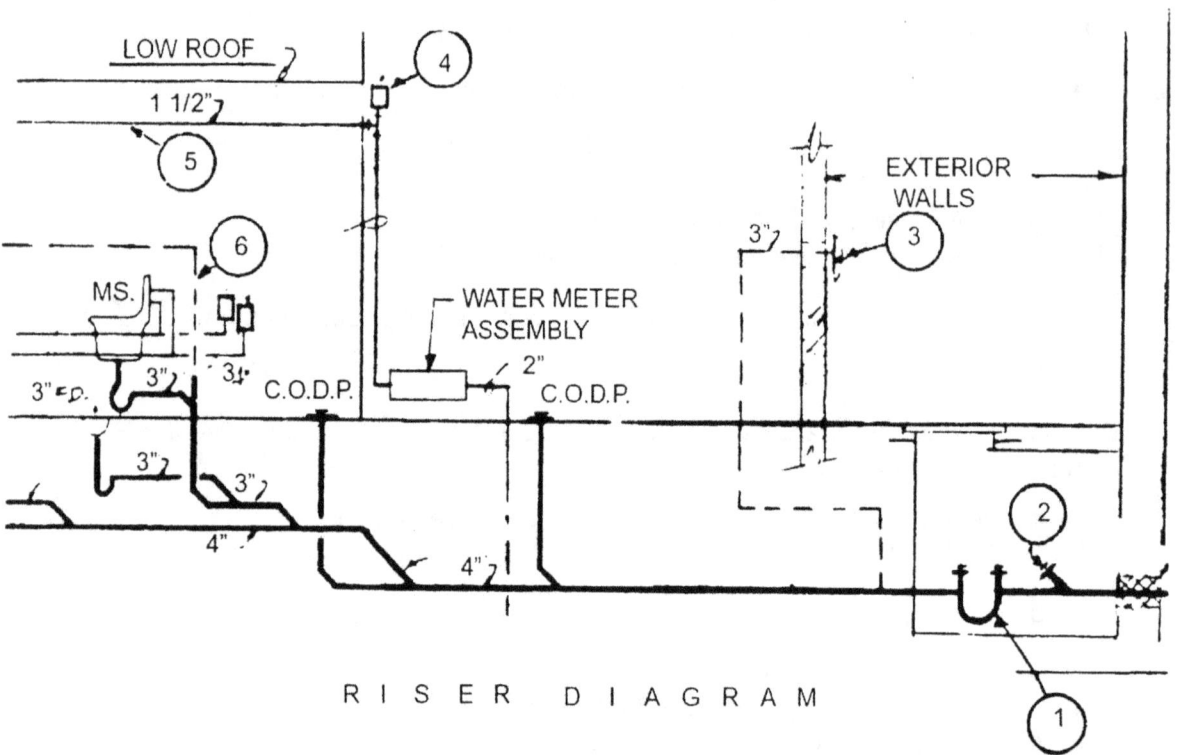

RISER DIAGRAM

34. Fitting 1 is a

   A. floor drain
   B. trap
   C. clean out
   D. check valve

35. Fitting 2 is a

   A. floor drain
   B. trap
   C. clean out
   D. check valve

36. Fitting 3 is a

   A. fire department connection
   B. sprinkler head
   C. valve
   D. fresh air inlet

37. Fitting 4 is a(n)

   A. gate valve
   B. air chamber
   C. running trap
   D. vent inlet

38. Line 5 is a

    A. hot water pipe
    B. vent line
    C. cold water line
    D. soil line

39. Line 6 is a _____ line.

    A. vent
    B. cold water
    C. hot water
    D. drain

40. A non-rising stem-type gate valve is especially useful when

    A. the stem must move downward only
    B. the pressure in the pipe must remain constant
    C. clearances around the valve are limited
    D. hand control of the valve is not required

KEY (CORRECT ANSWERS)

1. D	11. B	21. A	31. B
2. B	12. A	22. D	32. C
3. D	13. D	23. C	33. A
4. C	14. B	24. A	34. B
5. A	15. A	25. C	35. C
6. C	16. C	26. B	36. D
7. B	17. B	27. C	37. B
8. B	18. D	28. D	38. C
9. C	19. B	29. A	39. A
10. C	20. B	30. D	40. C

MECHANICAL APTITUDE EXAMINATION SECTION
TEST 1

MECHANICAL COMPREHENSION

DIRECTIONS: Questions 1 through 4 test your ability to understand general mechanical devices. Pictures are shown and questions asked about the mechanical devices shown in the picture. Read each question and study the picture. Each question is followed by four choices. For each question, choose the one BEST answer (A, B, C, or D). Then, *PRINT THE LETTER OF THE CORRECT ANSWER IN THE SPACE AT THE RIGHT.*

1.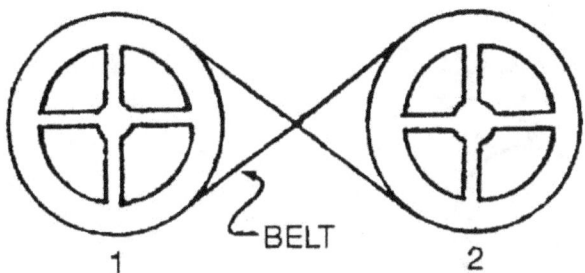

   The reason for crossing the belt connecting these wheels is to
   A. make the wheels turn in opposite directions
   B. make wheel 2 turn faster than wheel 1
   C. save wear on the belt
   D. take up slack in the belt

   1.____

2.

   The purpose of the small gear between the two large gears is to
   A. increase the speed of the larger gears
   B. allow the larger gears to turn in different directions
   C. decrease the speed of the larger gears
   D. make the larger gears turn in the same direction

   2.____

2 (#1)

3.

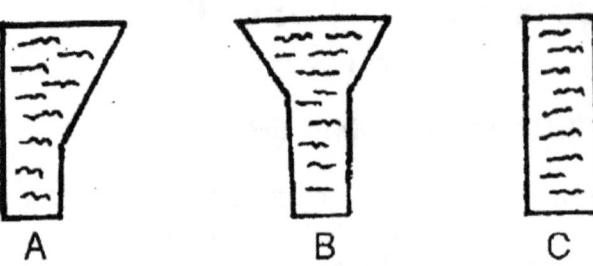

Each of these three-foot-high water cans have a bottom with an area of one square foot.
The pressure on the bottom of the cans is
   A. least in A   B. least in B   C. least in C   D. the same in all

4.

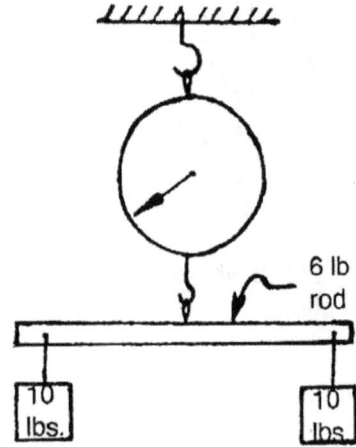

6 lb rod

The reading on the scale should be
   A. zero   B. 10 pounds   C. 13 pounds   D. 26 pounds

KEY (CORRECT ANSWERS)

1. A
2. D
3. D
4. D

TEST 2

DIRECTIONS: Questions 1 through 6 test knowledge of tools and how to use them. For each question, decide which one of the four things shown in the boxes labeled A, B, C, or D normally is used with or goes best with the thing in the picture on the left. *PRINT THE LETTER OF THE CORRECT ANSWER IN THE SPACE AT THE RIGHT.*

NOTE: All tools are NOT drawn to the same scale.

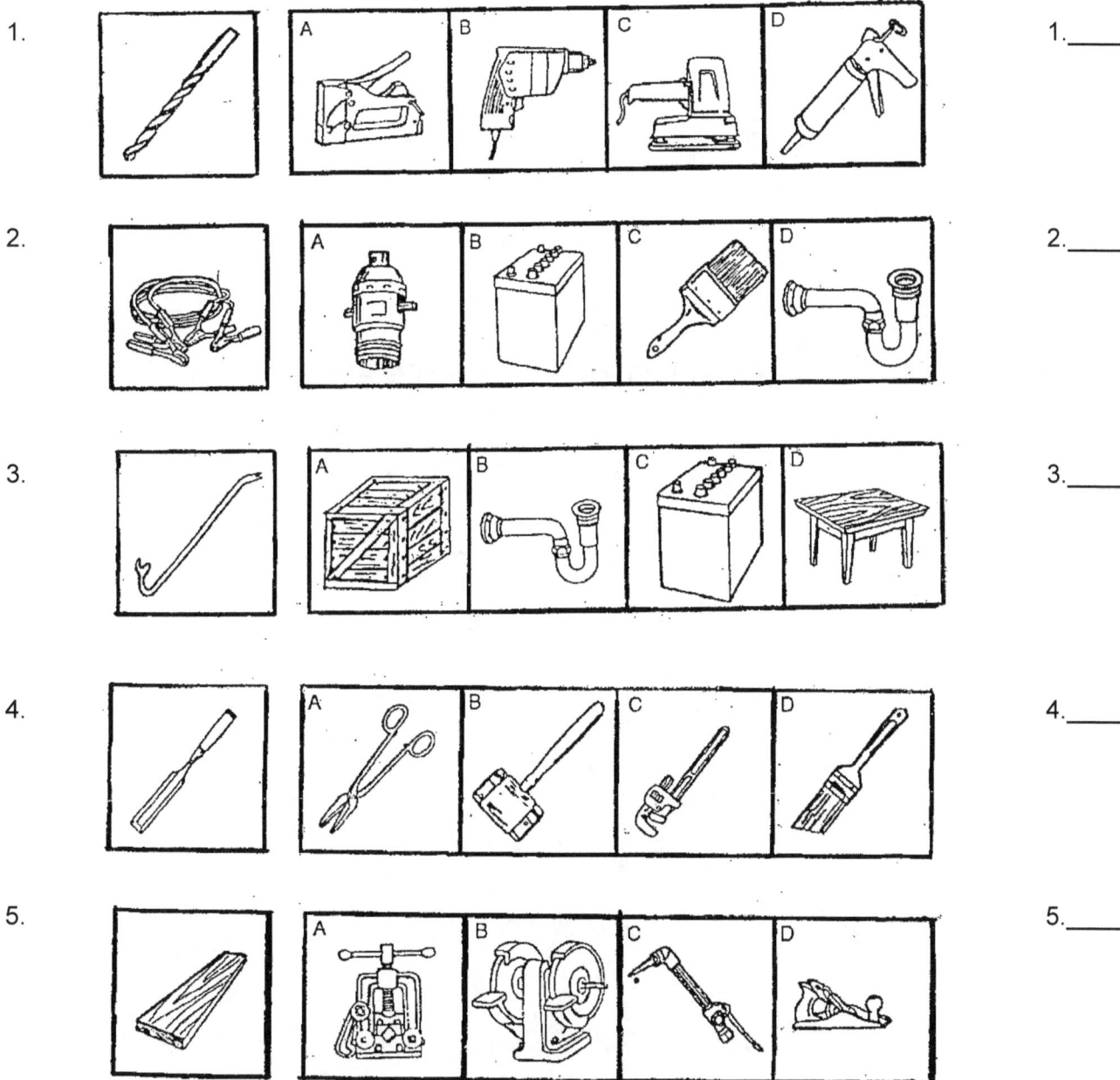

43

6.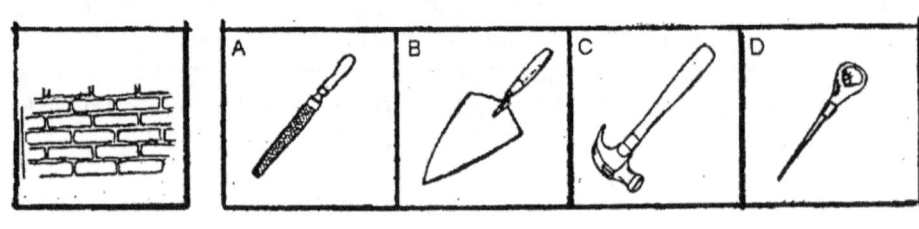

KEY (CORRECT ANSWERS)

1. B   4. B
2. B   5. D
3. A   6. B

MECHANICAL APTITUDE
Tools and Their Use

EXAMINATION SECTION
TEST 1

DIRECTIONS: Each question or incomplete statement is followed by several suggested answers or completions. Select the one that BEST answers the question or completes the statement. *PRINT THE LETTER OF THE CORRECT ANSWER IN THE SPACE AT THE RIGHT.*

Questions 1-10.

DIRECTIONS: Questions 1 through 10 refer to the tools shown below. The numbers in the answers refer to the numbers beneath the tools.
NOTE: These tools are NOT shown to scale.

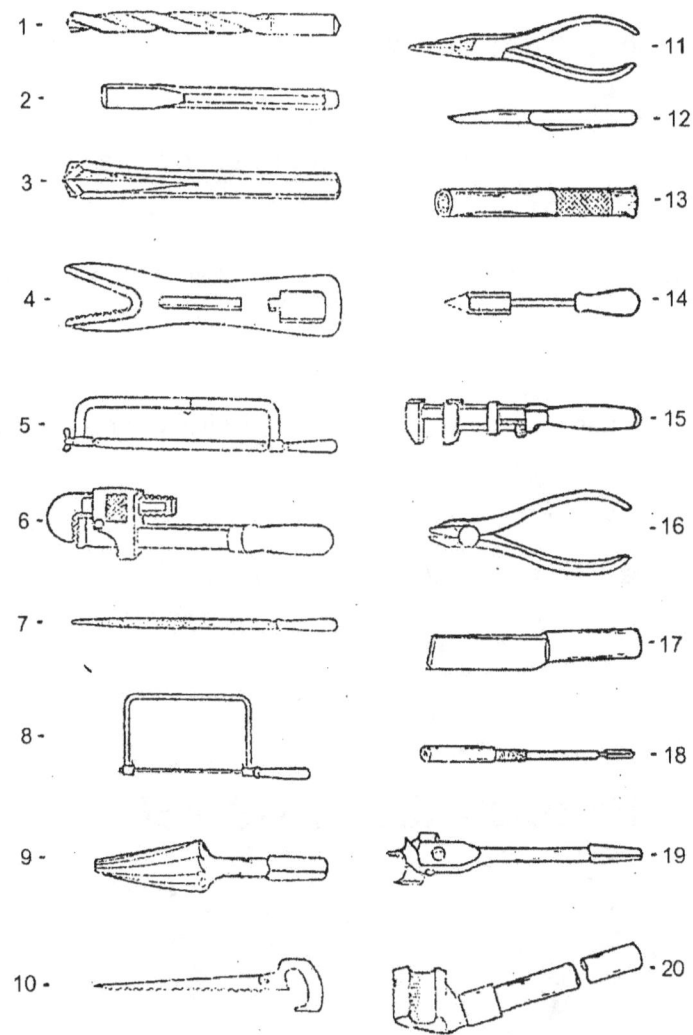

45

1. The tool that should be used for cutting a 1 7/8" diameter hole in a wood joist is number 1.____
   A. 3   B. 9   C. 14   D. 19

2. The tool that should be used for cutting thin-wall steel conduit is number qq 2.____
   A. 5   B. 8   C. 10   D. 16

3. The tool that should be used for soldering splices in electrical wire is number 3.____
   A. 3   B. 7   C. 13   D. 14

4. After cutting off a piece of a 3/4" diameter electrical conduit, the tool that should be used for removing a burr from the inside of the conduit is number 4.____
   A. 9   B. 11   C. 12   D. 14

5. The tool that should be used for turning a coupling onto a threaded conduit is number 5.____
   A. 6   B. 11   C. 15   D. 16

6. The tool that should be used for cutting wood lathing in plaster walls is number 6.____
   A. 5   B. 7   C. 10   D. 12

7. The tool that should be used for drilling a 3/8" diameter hole in a steel beam is number 7.____
   A. 1   B. 2   C. 3   D. 9

8. Of the following, the BEST tool to use for stripping insulation from electrical hook-up wire is number 8.____
   A. 11   B. 12   C. 15   D. 20

9. The tool that should be used for bending an electrical wire around a terminal post is number 9.____
   A. 4   B. 11   C. 15   D. 16

10. The tool that should be used for cutting electrical hook-up wire is number 10.____
    A. 5   B. 12   C. 16   D. 17

KEY (CORRECT ANSWERS)

1. D   6. C
2. A   7. A
3. D   8. B
4. A   9. B
5. A   10. C

TEST 2

DIRECTIONS: Each question or incomplete statement is followed by several suggested answers or completions. Select the one that BEST answers the question or completes the statement. *PRINT THE LETTER OF THE CORRECT ANSWER IN THE SPACE AT THE RIGHT.*

1. Round-nose pliers are *especially* useful for

    A. forming wire loops B. tightening small nuts
    C. crimping wires D. gripping small screws

2. A slight coating of rust on small tools is BEST removed by

    A. rubbing the tool with a dry cloth
    B. scraping the tool with a sharp knife
    C. scraping the tool with a small file having vaseline on it
    D. rubbing the tool with fine steel wool moistened with kerosene

3. The stake that should be used for hand-forming a small sheet metal cone is a _____ stake.

    A. hatchet B. bottom C. solid mandrel D. blowhorn

4. Of the following types of pliers, the BEST one to use to clamp down sheet metal to the top of a work bench is the

    A. channel-lock B. vise grip C. slip-joint D. duck bill

5. Angle brackets for supporting ductwork are *commonly* anchored to concrete walls by means of _____ bolts.

    A. carriage B. J- C. expansion D. foot

6. Of the following bolts, the *one* that should be used when attaching a hanger to a wooden joist is a _____ bolt.

    A. dead B. lag C. dardalet D. toggle

7. When bending sheet metal by hand, the BEST tool to use is a

    A. hand groover B. hand seamer
    C. hand ball tooler D. hand plier

8. Of the following types of steel rivets of the same size, the STRONGEST is the _____ rivet.

    A. tinners' B. flathead C. roundhead
    D. countersunk

9. Of the following snips, the one that can cut relatively thick sheet metal with the LEAST effort is _____ snips.

    A. straight B. aviation C. duck bill D. hawk bill

47

10. Of the following, the BEST tool to use to make a hole in a concrete floor for a machine hold-down bolt is a

    A. counterboring tool B. cold chisel
    C. drift punch D. star drill

11. Of the following, the BEST type of saw to use to cut a 4" diameter hole through a 5/8" wooden partition is a _____ saw.

    A. back B. saber C. circular D. cross-cut

12. While using a hacksaw to cut through a 1" diameter steel bar, a helper should not press down too heavily on the hacksaw because this may

    A. break the blade B. overheat the bar
    C. permanently distort the frame
    D. cause the hacksaw to slip

13. A miter box is used

    A. for locating dowel holes in two pieces of wood to be joined together
    B. to hold a saw at a fixed angle while sawing
    C. to hold a saw while sharpening its teeth
    D. to clamp two pieces of wood together at 90 degrees

14. Wing nuts are *especially* useful on equipment where

    A. the nuts must be removed frequently and easily
    B. the nuts are locked in place with a cotter pin
    C. critical adjustments are to be made frequently
    D. a standard hex head wrench cannot be used

15. The BEST device to employ to make certain that two points, separated by an unobstructed vertical distance of 12 feet, are in the best possible vertical alignment is a

    A. carpenter's square B. level
    C. folding ruler D. plumb bob

16. In a shop, snips should be used to

    A. hold small parts steady while machining them
    B. cut threaded pipe
    C. cut thin gauge sheet metal
    D. remove nuts that are seized on a bolt

17. A clutch is a device that is used

    A. to hold a work piece in a fixture
    B. for retrieving small parts from hard-to-reach areas
    C. to disengage one rotating shaft from another
    D. to level machinery on a floor

18. Of the following, the BEST device to use to determine whether the surface of a work bench is horizontal is a

    A. surface gage B. spirit level
    C. dial vernier D. profilometer

19. Of the following, the machine screw having the SMALLEST diameter is the   19.____

    A. 10-24 x 3/4"   B. 6-32 x 1 1/4"
    C. 12-24 x 1"   D. 8-32 x 1 1/2"

20. To close off one opening in a pipe tee when the line connecting into it is to be temporarily   20.____
    removed, it is necessary to use a

    A. pipe cap   B. pipe plug   C. nipple   D. bushing

21. The tool that should be used to cut a 1" x 4" plank down to a 3" width is a _____ saw.   21.____

    A. hack   B. crosscut   C. rip   D. back

22. Sharpening a hand saw consists of four major steps, *namely*,   22.____

    A. jointing, shaping, setting and filing
    B. adzing, clinching, forging and machining
    C. brazing, chiseling, grinding and mitering
    D. bushing, dressing, lapping, and machining

23. If it is necessary to shorten the length of a bolt by cutting through the threaded portion,   23.____
    the SIMPLEST procedure to avoid difficulty with the thread is to

    A. cut parallel to the threads in the groove of the thread
    B. run on a die after cutting
    C. turn on a nut past the cutting point prior to cutting
    D. clear the injured thread with a 3-cornered file

24. The wrench that would prove LEAST useful in uncoupling several pieces of pipe is a   24.____
    _____ wrench.

    A. socket   B. chain   C. strap   D. stillson

25. Gaskets are *commonly* used between the flanges of large pipe joints to   25.____

    A. provide space for assembly
    B. take up expansion and contraction
    C. prevent the flanges from rusting together
    D. make a tight connection

KEY (CORRECT ANSWERS)

1. A
2. D
3. D
4. B
5. C

6. B
7. B
8. C
9. B
10. D

11. B
12. A
13. B
14. A
15. D

16. C
17. C
18. B
19. B
20. B

21. C
22. A
23. C
24. A
25. D

SAFETY
EXAMINATION SECTION
TEST 1

DIRECTIONS: Each question or incomplete statement is followed by several suggested answers or completions. Select the one that BEST answers the question or completes the statement. *PRINT THE LETTER OF THE COREECT ANSWER IN THE SPACE AT THE RIGHT.*

1. When carrying pipe, employees are cautioned against lifting with the fingers inserted in the ends.
   The PROBABLE reason for this caution is to avoid the possibility of

   A. dropping and damaging pipe
   B. getting dirt and perspiration on the inside of the pipe
   C. cutting the fingers on the edge of the pipe
   D. straining finger muscles

   1.____

2. The MOST common cause for a workman to lose his balance and fall when working from an extension ladder is

   A. too much spring in the ladder
   B. sideways sliding of the top
   C. exerting a heavy pull on an object which gives suddenly
   D. working on something directly behind the ladder

   2.____

3. It is NOT necessary to wear protective goggles when

   A. drilling rivet holes in a steel beam
   B. sharpening tools on a power grinder
   C. welding a steel plate to a pipe column
   D. laying up a cinder block partition

   3.____

4. On your first day on the job as a helper, you are assigned to work with a maintainer. During the course of the work, you realize that the maintainer is about to violate a basic safety rule.
   In this case, the BEST thing for you to do is to

   A. immediately call it to his attention
   B. say nothing until he actually violates the rule and then call it to his attention
   C. say nothing, but later report this action to the foreman
   D. walk away from him so that you will not become involved

   4.____

5. Telephones are located alongside of the tracks for emergency use. The locations of these telephones are indicated by blue lights.
   The reason for selecting this color rather than green is that

   A. a blue light can be seen for greater distances
   B. blue lights are easier to buy
   C. green cannot be seen by a person who is color-blind
   D. green lights are used for train signals

   5.____

6. If it is necessary to lift up and hold one heavy part of a piece of equipment with a pinch bar so that there is enough clearance to work with the hands under the part, one IMPORTANT precaution is to

   A. wear gloves
   B. watch the bar to be ready if it slips
   C. work as fast as possible
   D. insert a temporary block to hold the part

7. The MOST important reason for insisting on neatness in maintenance quarters is that it

   A. increases the available storage space
   B. makes for good employee morale
   C. prevents tools from becoming rusty
   D. decreases the chances of accidents to employees

8. There are many steel ladders and stairways for the use of maintenance workers. Their GREATEST danger is that they

   A. have sharp edges causing cuts
   B. are slippery when greasy and wet
   C. cause colds
   D. have no *give* and thus cause fatigue

9. When using a brace and bit to bore a hole completely through a partition, it is MOST important to

   A. lean heavily on the brace and bit
   B. maintain a steady turning speed all through the job
   C. have the body in a position that will not be easily thrown off balance
   D. reverse the direction of the bit at frequent intervals

10. Flux is used when soldering two pieces of sheet metal together in order to

    A. conduct the heat of the soldering iron to the sheets
    B. lower the melting point of the solder
    C. glue the solder to the sheets
    D. protect the sheet metal from oxidizing when heated by the soldering iron

11. A rule of the transit system states that in walking on the track, walk opposite the direction of traffic on that track if possible.
    By logical reasoning, the PRINCIPAL safety idea behind this rule is that the man on the track

    A. is more likely to see an approaching train
    B. will be seen more readily by the motorman
    C. need not be as careful
    D. is better able to judge the speed of the train

12. An outstanding cause of accidents is the improper use of tools.
    The MOST helpful conclusion you can draw from this statement is that

    A. most tools are defective
    B. many accidents involving the use of tools occur because of poor working habits

C. most workers are poorly trained
D. many accidents involving the use of tools are unavoidable

13. An employee is required to make a written report of any unusual occurrence promptly. The BEST reason for requiring promptness is that

    A. it helps prevent similar occurrences
    B. the employee is less likely to forget details
    C. there is always a tendency to do a better job under pressure
    D. the report may be too long if made at an employee"s convenience

14. There are a few workers who are seemingly prone to accidents and who, regardless of their assigned job, have a higher accident rate than the average worker.
    If your co-worker is known to be such an individual, the BEST course for you to pursue would be to

    A. do most of the assigned work yourself
    B. refuse to work with this individual
    C. provide him with a copy of all rules and regulations
    D. personally check all safety precautions on each job

15. When summoning an ambulance for an injured person, it is MOST important to give the

    A. name of the injured person
    B. nature of the injuries
    C. cause of the accident
    D. location of the injured person

16. The MOST likely cause of accidents involving minor injuries is

    A. careless work practices
    B. lack of safety devices
    C. inferior equipment and materials
    D. insufficient safety posters

17. In an accident report, the information which may be MOST useful in decreasing the recurrence of similar-type accidents is the

    A. extent of injuries sustained
    B. time the accident happened
    C. number of people involved
    D. cause of the accident

18. Before a newly-riveted connection can be approved, the rivets should be struck with a light hammer in order to

    A. improve the shape of the rivet heads
    B. knock off any rust or burnt metal
    C. detect any loose rivets
    D. give the rivets a tighter fit

19. If the feet of a ladder are found to be resting on a slightly uneven surface, it would be BEST to

    A. move the ladder to an entirely different location
    B. even up the feet of the ladder with a small wedge
    C. get two men to bolster the ladder while it is being climbed
    D. get another ladder that is more suitable to the conditions

20. It would be POOR practice to hold a piece of wood in your hands or lap while you are tightening a screw in the wood because

    A. the wood would probably split
    B. sufficient leverage cannot be obtained
    C. the screwdriver may bend
    D. you might injure yourself

21. If a man on a job has to report an accident to the office by telephone, he should request the name of the person taking the call and also note the time.
    The reason for this precaution is to fix responsibility for the

    A. entire handling of the accident thereafter
    B. accuracy of the report
    C. recording of the report
    D. preparation of the final written report

22. Employees of the transit system whose work requires them to enter upon the tracks are warned not to wear loose-fitting clothes.
    The MOST important reason for this warning is that loose-fitting clothes may

    A. tear more easily than snug-fitting clothes
    B. give insufficient protection against dust
    C. catch on some projection of a passing train
    D. interfere when the men are using heavy tools

23. In case of accident, employees who witnessed the accident are required to make INDIVIDUAL written reports on prescribed forms as soon as possible.
    The MOST logical reason for requiring such individual reports rather than a single, joint report signed by all witnesses is that the individual reports are

    A. *less* likely to be lost at the same time
    B. *more* likely to result in reducing the number of accidents
    C. *less* likely to contain unnecessary information
    D. *more* likely to give the complete picture

24. The logical reason that certain employees who work on the tracks carry small parts in fiber pails rather than in steel pails is that fiber pails

    A. can't be dented by rough usage
    B. do not conduct electricity
    C. are stronger
    D. can't rust

25. Maintenance workers whose duties require them to work on the tracks generally work in pairs.
 The LEAST likely of the following possible reasons for this practice is that

    A. the men can help each other in case of accident
    B. it protects against vandalism
    C. some of the work requires two men
    D. there is usually too much equipment for one man to carry

25.____

KEY (CORRECT ANSWERS)

1.	C	11.	A
2.	C	12.	B
3.	D	13.	B
4.	A	14.	D
5.	D	15.	D
6.	D	16.	A
7.	D	17.	D
8.	B	18.	C
9.	C	19.	B
10.	D	20.	D

21. C
22. C
23. D
24. B
25. B

TEST 2

DIRECTIONS: Each question or incomplete statement is followed by several suggested answers or completions. Select the one that BEST answers the question or completes the statement. *PRINT THE LETTER OF THE CORRECT ANSWER IN THE SPACE AT THE RIGHT.*

1. Safety-mindedness cannot be achieved by command; it must be developed. Assume that you will be responsible for informing and training your subordinates in proper safety procedures.
   Which of the following methods is the MOST effective means of developing proper concern for safety among your subordinates?

   A. Award prizes for the best safety slogans
   B. Issue monthly safety bulletins
   C. Establish a safety suggestion program
   D. Hold periodic, informal group meetings on safety

2. Of the following, the MAIN purpose of a safety training program for employees is to

   A. fix the blame for accidents
   B. describe accidents which have occurred
   C. hold the employees responsible for unsafe working conditions
   D. make the employees aware of the basic causes of accidents

3. When administering first aid to a person suffering from shock as a result of an accident, of the following, it is MOST important to

   A. cover the person and keep him warm
   B. apply artificial respiration
   C. prop him up in a sitting position
   D. massage the person in order to aid blood circulation

4. Assume you have just been appointed. You notice that certain equipment which is assigned to you is defective and that use of this equipment may eventually result in unnecessary costs and perhaps injury to you.
   The BEST thing for you to do is to

   A. speak to the maintenance men in the project about repairing the equipment
   B. discuss the matter with your foreman
   C. mind your own business since you have just been appointed
   D. speak to other workers and find out if they had any experience with defective equipment

5. Assume you are working in a project building and one of the housing caretakers has just been seriously injured in an accident in the slop sink room.
   Your FIRST concern should be to

   A. help the injured man
   B. find the cause of the accident
   C. report the accident to your foreman
   D. report the accident to the caretaker's boss

6. Assume a mass of extension cords plugged into one outlet in a shop results in overloading the electrical circuit and causes a fire.
   Which of the following types of extinguisher should be used to put out the fire?

   A. Carbon dioxide (CO_2)
   B. Water
   C. Soda acid
   D. Carbon tetrachloride

   6.____

7. Manufacturers of chemicals usually recommend that special precautions be taken when the chemicals are used.
   Of the following, which one would a manufacturer be LEAST likely to recommend?

   A. Wear leather gloves
   B. Wear a respirator
   C. Wear safety goggles
   D. Have a first aid kit available

   7.____

Questions 8-10.

DIRECTIONS: Questions 8 through 10 consist of groups of statements that have to do with safety precautions and procedures. Choose the statement in each group that is NOT correct.

8. A. The label on the original container of the pesticide should be read before each use.
    B. Pest control equipment should be cleaned regularly.
    C. Whenever there is a choice of chemicals, the chemical which is less hazardous to humans should be used at all times.
    D. For the transfer of concentrates from drums, either threaded taps or drum pumps should be used.

    8.____

9. A. Do not use a petroleum base on an asphalt tile floor.
    B. Do not spray oil base sprays on material colored with oil soluble dyes.
    C. Do not use respirators.
    D. Do not use pesticides which are highly poisonous to mammals.

    9.____

10. (The following statements deal with disposal of empty containers which hold highly toxic organic phosphate insecticides.)

    A. Do not reuse these containers.
    B. Pour one pint of water into the empty container, add bicarbonate of soda, and bury the container of rinse solution at least 18 inches below ground.
    C. Wet all inner surfaces with the proper rinse solution.
    D. Punch holes in the top and bottom of the can, crush the can, and bury deeply in an isolated location.

    10.____

11. A good first-aid treatment to administer to a man who has apparently been rendered unconscious by a high voltage shock would be to

    A. give him a stimulant by mouth
    B. apply artificial respiration if he is not breathing
    C. apply artificial respiration as a precautionary measure even if he is breathing
    D. keep him warm and comfortable

    11.____

12. A contributing cause present in practically all accidents is

    A. failure to give close attention to the job at hand
    B. lack of cooperation among the men in a gang
    C. failure to place the right man in the right job
    D. use of improper tools

13. Safety requires that wood ladders be unpainted.
    The PROBABLE reason for this is that paint

    A. is inflammable
    B. may deteriorate wood
    C. makes ladder rungs slippery
    D. may cover cracks or defects

14. If you notice one of your helpers doing a job in an unsafe manner and he tells you that this is the way the maintainer told him to do it, you should FIRST

    A. speak to this maintainer and find out if the helper was telling you the truth
    B. reprimand the helper for violating safety rules
    C. question this maintainer to see if he knows the safe way to do the job
    D. show the helper the correct method and see that he does the job properly

15. If a person has a deep puncture in his finger caused by a sharp nail, the BEST immediate first-aid procedure would be to

    A. encourage bleeding by exerting pressure around the injured area
    B. stop all bleeding
    C. prevent air from reaching the wound
    D. probe the wound for steel particles

16. It is MOST important to give complete details of an accident on the accident report because this will

    A. cause the injured employee to be more careful in the future
    B. keep supervision informed of the working conditions
    C. help in the defense against spurious compensation claims
    D. provide information to help avoid future accidents

17. A transit employee equipped with only a white flashlight, who wishes to stop a train because of an emergency, should face the train and wave the light in a

    A. vertical line
    B. vertical circle
    C. horizontal line
    D. forward and backward direction

18. The employee who opens a first-aid kit must make an immediate report on a prescribed form.
    Such report would NOT show the

    A. name of the employee opening the kit
    B. last previous date on which the kit was used

C. purpose for which the materials therein were used
D. amount of first aid material used

19. Carbon tetrachloride fire extinguishers have been replaced by dry chemical fire extinguishers MAINLY because the carbon tetrachloride is

   A. toxic
   B. not as effective
   C. frequently pilfered for cleaning purposes
   D. not readily available

20. The BEST first-aid for a man who has no external injury but is apparently suffering from internal injury due to an accident is to

   A. take him immediately to a doctor's office
   B. administer a stimulant
   C. cover him with a blanket and immediately summon a doctor or ambulance
   D. administer artificial respiration

21. While your men were working on the plumbing of a station toilet, a passenger tripped over some of your material on the platform.
    In making a report of the accident, the LEAST necessary item to include is the

   A. time of day
   B. distance from the entrance turnstile to the toilet
   C. date of occurrence
   D. condition of the platform when the accident occurred

22. All employees witnessing an accident are required to make a written report as soon as possible describing what they witnessed.
    The MOST likely reason for requiring these reports in writing and as soon as possible is to

   A. make sure no witnesses are overlooked
   B. be able to correct the reports without delay
   C. get as many facts as possible on record before they are forgotten
   D. relieve supervision of the time consuming job of verbally questioning all witnesses

23. Of the following, the type of fire extinguisher which should be used on electrical fires is the _____ type.

   A. foam   B. soda-acid
   C. pumped-water   D. dry chemical

24. The PRIMARY purpose of an emergency alarm is to

   A. test circuits to see if they are alive
   B. provide a means of removing power from the third rail
   C. inform the trainmaster that trains cannot run in his zone
   D. inform maintenance crews working on the tracks that an emergency exists

25. In regard to flagging signals, which of the following statements is TRUE?

    A. A red flag must never be used to give a proceed signal to a motorman.
    B. Under all conditions, only a red flag or lamp can be used as a signal to the motorman to stop the train.
    C. After stopping a train, if a flagman wishes to signal the motorman to resume his normal speed, he should wave a yellow flag.
    D. Under normal flagging conditions, moving a white light up and down slowly is a signal to the motorman to resume normal speed and that the motorman should be prepared to stop within his range of vision.

KEY (CORRECT ANSWERS)

1.	D	11.	B
2.	D	12.	A
3.	A	13.	D
4.	B	14.	D
5.	A	15.	A
6.	A	16.	D
7.	A	17.	C
8.	C	18.	B
9.	C	19.	A
10.	B	20.	C

21. B
22. C
23. D
24. B
25. A

EXAMINATION SECTION
TEST 1

DIRECTIONS: Each question or incomplete statement is followed by several suggested answers or completions. Select the one that BEST answers the question or completes the statement. *PRINT THE LETTER OF THE CORRECT ANSWER IN THE SPACE AT THE RIGHT.*

1. The boiling point of water at 1 atmosphere pressure is 100 on the _____ scale.   1._____

   A. Baumé   B. Centigrade
   C. Fahrenheit   D. Kelvin

2. Ordinary atmospheric pressure on a mercury barometer is 76   2._____

   A. centimeters   B. inches
   C. feet   D. millimeters

3. The density of water is MOST NEARLY one   3._____

   A. gram per square centimeter
   B. kilogram per liter
   C. pound per quart
   D. pound per square inch

4. A round-bottomed flask is also called a _____ flask.   4._____

   A. boiling   B. Claisen
   C. Erlenmeyer   D. volumetric

5. The term *Buchner* refers to a type of   5._____

   A. condenser   B. crucible   C. funnel   D. tube

6. The term *Westphal* refers to a type of   6._____

   A. balance   B. burner   C. condenser   D. flask

7. The term *Nessler* refers to a type of   7._____

   A. balance   B. flask
   C. hydrometer   D. tube

8. Of the following, the one used to determine the freezing point of liquids is the   8._____

   A. calorimeter   B. cryoscope
   C. polariscope   D. pyenometer

9. Of the following, the one which is the DENSEST liquid is   9._____

   A. alcohol   B. benzene
   C. water   D. carbon tetrachloride

10. A Kipp generator is *generally* used to generate   10._____

    A. alternating current   B. direct current
    C. helium gas   D. hydrogen sulfide

61

11. The one of the following gases which is LIGHTER than air is

   A. ammonia
   B. bromine
   C. carbon dioxide
   D. oxygen

12. Of the following halogens, the one which has the LOWEST atomic weight is

   A. bromine   B. chlorine   C. fluorine   D. iodine

13. Small amounts of sodium left unreacted in the bottom of a flask are *generally* destroyed by

   A. adding absolute alcohol
   B. adding boiling water
   C. adding hot benzene
   D. heating to dull redness

14. The color of freshly prepared *cleaning solution* is

   A. blue   B. green   C. red   D. yellow

15. To assure delivery of the proper volume, a pipette marked *25 ml (Deliver)* should be allowed to empty,

   A. and then be immediately removed from the receiving vessel
   B. and then the last few drops should be blown out
   C. drained for 30 seconds, and then the last few drops should be blown out
   D. drained for 30 seconds, and then touched to the wall of the receiving vessel

16. The SAFEST way to heat a distilling flask containing ether is with a(n)

   A. electrical heater or hot plate
   B. oxygen-gas burner
   C. small Bunsen flame
   D. Wood's metal bath

17. Of the following laboratory procedures, the one which is MOST dangerous is adding

   A. alcohol to water
   B. concentrated sulfuric acid to water
   C. water to alcohol
   D. water to concentrated sulfuric acid

18. If $x^2 = 10^{-14}$, then x =

   A. 10^{-7} B. 10^{-12} C. 10^{-16} D. 10^{-28}

19. The normality of a solution of 0.10 molar acetic acid _____ normality of a 0.10 molar solution of HCl.

   A. bears no relation to the
   B. is higher than the
   C. is lower than the
   D. is the same as the

20. The average weighing error on the standard analytical balance is MOST NEARLY

   A. 0.02 grams
   B. 0.2 grams
   C. 0.2 milligrams
   D. 2 micrograms

21. The amount of 0.20 N NaOH which will EXACTLY neutralize 20 ml of 0.10 N HCl is _____ ml.

    A. 5 B. 10 C. 20 D. 40

21.____

22. Of the following, the one which is LEAST reactive is

    A. argon B. chlorine C. hydrogen D. nitrogen

22.____

23. Of the following, the one which is a STRONG oxidizing agent is

    A. argon B. chlorine C. hydrogen D. nitrogen

23.____

24. Of the following metals, the one with the LOWEST density is

    A. aluminum B. copper C. iron D. zinc

24.____

25. A weighted sample of an unknown metal is dissolved in dilute acid and the volume of evolved hydrogen, dried and reduced to STP is determined.
    This information is *sufficient* to determine the metal's

    A. atomic number
    C. equivalent weight
    B. atomic weight
    D. molecular weight

25.____

KEY (CORRECT ANSWERS)

1. B		11. A	
2. A		12. C	
3. B		13. A	
4. A		14. C	
5. C		15. D	
6. A		16. A	
7. D		17. D	
8. B		18. A	
9. D		19. D	
10. D		20. C	

21. B
22. A
23. B
24. A
25. C

TEST 2

DIRECTIONS: Each question or incomplete statement is followed by several suggested answers or completions. Select the one that BEST answers the question or completes the statement. *PRINT THE LETTER OF THE CORRECT ANSWER IN THE SPACE AT THE RIGHT.*

1. The weight percent of hydrogen in water is MOST NEARLY 1.____
   A. 5.9   B. 11.1   C. 33.3   D. 50.0

2. Of the following, the instrument used to measure the density of an unknown liquid is the 2.____
   A. ebullioscope
   B. polarimeter
   C. pycnometer
   D. viscosimeter

3. Of the following, the one which is an indicator *commonly* used in acid-base titrations is 3.____
   A. indigo
   B. methyl red
   C. silver chromate
   D. tetramethyl ammonium chloride

4. A solution of one mole of cane sugar in 1000 gms of water 4.____
   A. freezes at a higher temperature than pure water
   B. freezes at a lower temperature than pure water
   C. freezes at the same temperature as pure water
   D. will not freeze at all

5. The vacuum bottle or thermos bottle is also called the _____ flask. 5.____
   A. Dewar
   B. Erlenmeyer
   C. Florence
   D. Wolff

6. The gram-molecular weight of hydrogen gas is _____ gms. 6.____
   A. 0.0084   B. 1.008   C. 2.016   D. 22.4

7. An electron has a 7.____
   A. charge depending on the atomic number
   B. negative charge
   C. positive charge
   D. zero charge

8. Elements with the same atomic number but different atomic weights are called 8.____
   A. isentropes
   B. isobars
   C. isomers
   D. isotopes

9. A mole of helium gas has a volume, at standard temperature and pressure, of _____ liter(s). 9.____
   A. 1   B. 11.2   C. 22.4   D. 44.8

64

10. If 100 ml of a gas at standard temperature and pressure is changed to a pressure of 1520 mm Hg and a temperature of 273° C, its volume

    A. is changed to 50 ml
    B. is changed to 200 ml
    C. is changed to 400 ml
    D. remains unchanged

11. The extraction of I_2 from 100 ml of a water solution is performed MOST efficiently by

    A. one 50-ml portion of CCl_4
    B. one 50-ml portion of ethanol
    C. five 10-ml portions of CCl_4
    D. five 10-ml portions of ethanol

12. The RECOMMENDED way of making a U-shaped bend in 8 mm soft glass tubing is

    A. by wrapping with nichrome wire and heating electrically
    B. in a Bunsen flame
    C. in an acetylene-oxygen blast lamp
    D. in an oxyhydrogen blast lamp

13. Fire-polishing removes

    A. cloudiness from devitrified glass
    B. etching from the bottom of flasks and beakers
    C. rough edges from glass tubing
    D. scratches and abrasions from glass

14. One inch is APPROXIMATELY _____ mm.

    A. 0.025   B. 0.25   C. 2.5   D. 25

15. One liter is APPROXIMATELY

    A. 1 pint   B. 1 quart   C. 2 quarts   D. 1 gallon

16. Of the following gases, the ONLY one which can be collected by the upward displacement of air is

    A. CO_2 B. H_2 C. NO_2 D. SO_2

17. Of the following gases, the one which is MOST poisonous is

    A. CO_2 B. H_2 C. H_2S D. N_2O

18. Of the following gases, the one which has a noticeable color is

    A. NH_3 B. NO   C. NO_2 D. N_2O

19. Of the following, the one with the HIGHEST boiling point is

    A. HCl   B. HNO_3 C. H_2O D. H_2SO_4

20. Of the following, the one with the HIGHEST melting point is

    A. acetone   B. hydrogen   C. mercury   D. water

21. pH is defined as the   21.____

   A. [H⁺]   B. log [H⁺]   C. -log [H⁺]   D. log (10[H⁺])

22. A Wheatstone bridge is used for   22.____

   A. connecting glass to rubber
   B. holding a funnel over a beaker
   C. measuring hardness
   D. measuring electrical resistances

23. Of the following substances, the one which is MOST inflammable is   23.____

   A. CCl_4 B. $CHCl_3$ C. Cl_2 D. Na_2CO_3

24. One pound is APPROXIMATELY _____ grams.   24.____

   A. 0.065   B. 28.3   C. 454   D. 1000

25. A catalyst is a substance which   25.____

   A. changes the point of equilibrium of a reaction
   B. increases the dissociation of weak acids
   C. increases the rate of a reaction
   D. reacts with undesired products of a reaction

KEY (CORRECT ANSWERS)

1.	B	11.	C
2.	C	12.	B
3.	B	13.	C
4.	B	14.	D
5.	A	15.	B
6.	C	16.	B
7.	B	17.	C
8.	D	18.	C
9.	C	19.	D
10.	D	20.	D

21. C
22. D
23. B
24. C
25. C

EXAMINATION SECTION
TEST 1

DIRECTIONS: Each question or incomplete statement is followed by several suggested answers or completions. Select the one that BEST answers the question or completes the statement. *PRINT THE LETTER OF THE CORRECT ANSWER IN THE SPACE AT THE RIGHT.*

NOTE: The following list of atomic weights may be referred to in solving problems involving computations:

Chlorine	35.5	Hydrogen	1.0	Silver	107.9
Chromium	52.0	Nitrogen	14.0	Sodium	23.0
Copper	63.5	Oxygen	16.0	Sulfur	32.0

1. Sulfuric acid is an example of a _____ acid.
   - A. monoprotic
   - B. diprotic
   - C. tetraprotic
   - D. triprotic

2. A solution with a pH of 7.5 is *generally* considered to be
   - A. strongly acidic
   - B. strongly basic
   - C. weakly acidic
   - D. weakly basic

3. Of the following acids, the one which is considered to be the WEAKEST is _____ acid.
   - A. nitric
   - B. perchloric
   - C. phosphoric
   - D. sulfuric

4. Of the following elements, the one NOT classified as an *inert gas* is
   - A. helium
   - B. neon
   - C. plutonium
   - D. radon

5. The absolute temperature scale is also known as the _____ scale.
   - A. Celsius
   - B. Centigrade
   - C. Fahrenheit
   - D. Kelvin

6. Atoms whose nuclei contain the same number of protons but different numbers of neutrons are called
   - A. allotropes
   - B. isomers
   - C. isotopes
   - D. polymers

7. A colloidal system in which one liquid is dispersed in another liquid is termed a(n)
   - A. emulsion
   - B. foam
   - C. fog
   - D. suspension

8. The burning of fuel in air is an example of a reaction called
   - A. endothermic
   - B. exothermic
   - C. thermophilic
   - D. thermoduric

9. Of the following metals, the one which is MOST active is
   - A. iron
   - B. lead
   - C. potassium
   - D. zinc

10. Of the following metals, the one which is LEAST active is

    A. aluminum   B. copper   C. nickel   D. silver

11. Of the following, the element which is a liquid at standard conditions (0° C and 1 atm) is

    A. arsenic   B. barium   C. iodine   D. mercury

12. According to modern concepts, every atom consists of

    A. one electron and one nucleus
    B. one electron and one or more nuclei
    C. one nucleus and one or more electrons
    D. more than one nucleus and more than one electron

13. According to modern nuclear chemistry, the one of the following which is NOT a fundamental particle is the

    A. betatron   B. meson   C. positron   D. proton

14. The Einstein equation which shows the relation of mass to energy is

    A. $E = mc$ B. $E = mc^2$ C. $E = m^2c$ D. $E^2 = mc$

15. A liter may be defined as the volume of a kilogram of water at _____ ° C.

    A. 0   B. 4   C. 20   D. 100

16. 0.6024×10^{24} is known as

    A. Avogadro's number   B. Bohr's number
    C. Boltzmann's constant   D. Planck's constant

17. The formula for hypochlorous acid is

    A. $HClO$ B. $HClO_2$ C. $HClO_3$ D. $HClO_4$

18. The chemical name for slaked line is calcium

    A. carbonate   B. hydroxide   C. nitride   D. oxide

19. The chemical name for baking soda is sodium

    A. carbonate   B. chloride
    C. hydrogen carbonate   D. hydroxide

20. The chemical symbol W stands for

    A. plutonium   B. tungsten
    C. vanadium   D. white phosphorus

21. Sodium sulfate is an example of a(n) _____ salt.

    A. acid   B. basic   C. double   D. normal

22. Brass is essentially an alloy of copper and

    A. aluminum   B. antimony   C. nickel   D. zinc

23. The number 1,000,000, expressed in the exponential form, is 1 x   23.____

    A. 10^5 B. 10^6 C. 10^7 D. 10^8

24. 10^3 x 10^3 equals   24.____

    A. 10   B. 10^3 C. 10^6 D. 10^9

25. CHEMICAL ABSTRACTS is published by the   25.____

    A. American Chemical Society
    B. American Society of Chemical Engineers
    C. Association of Official Agricultural Chemists
    D. National Bureau of Standards

KEY (CORRECT ANSWERS)

1.	B	11.	D
2.	D	12.	C
3.	C	13.	A
4.	C	14.	B
5.	D	15.	B
6.	C	16.	A
7.	A	17.	A
8.	B	18.	B
9.	C	19.	C
10.	D	20.	B

21. D
22. D
23. B
24. C
25. A

TEST 2

DIRECTIONS: Each question or incomplete statement is followed by several suggested answers or completions. Select the one that BEST answers the question or completes the statement. *PRINT THE LETTER OF THE CORRECT ANSWER IN THE SPACE AT THE RIGHT.*

1. At constant temperature, the pressure of a gas varies inversely with the volume. If K represents a coefficient depending only one the temperature, then   1.___

    A. P=KV   B. P = K/V   C. P = V/K   D. 1/P = K x 1/V

2. *Dry Ice* is solid   2.___

    A. carbon dioxide   B. freon
    C. neon   D. nitrous oxide

3. Of the following elements, the one which is NOT a gas at standard conditions (0°C and 1 atm) is   3.___

    A. bromine   B. chlorine   C. fluorine   D. helium

4. Aniline is classed as an   4.___

    A. inorganic acid   B. inorganic base
    C. organic acid   D. organic base

5. The molecular weight of nitrous acid is APPROXIMATELY   5.___

    A. 31   B. 47   C. 63   D. 79

Questions 6-13.

DIRECTIONS: Systematic analysis of a solution for metallic ions consists initially in dividing the ions up into groups. Column I lists positive ions, each of which can be placed with one of the analytical groups in Column II. For each ion in Column I, write in the space at the right the letter in front of the group in Column II to which it belongs.

COLUMN I	COLUMN II	
6. Bi^{+++}	A. Alkali group	6.___
7. Ca^{++}	B. Silver group	7.___
8. Cr^{+++}	C. Copper-Arsenic group	8.___
9. Hg_2^{++}	D. Aluminum-Zinc group	9.___
10. K^+	E. Alkaline Earth group	10.___
11. Mn^{++}		11.___
12. NH_4^+		12.___
13. Sn^{++}		13.___

14. The color of PbCrO$_4$ formed in the confirmatory test for Pb^{++} is

    A. black   B. brown   C. white   D. yellow

15. The color of ZnS formed in the confirmatory test for Zn^{++} is

    A. black   B. brown   C. orange   D. white

16. The halogen compound of Pb^{++} which is MOST soluble in water is the

    A. bromide   B. chloride   C. fluoride   D. iodide

17. Dimethylglyoxime is generally used as confirmatory test for

    A. Al^{+++} B. Co^{++} C. Fe^{++} D. Ni^{++}

18. The color of the lake formed when using aluminon in the confirmatory test for Al^{+++} is

    A. blue   B. green   C. red   D. white

19. The chloride ion is the reagent used for the separation of the _____ group from the other groups.

    A. alkaline earth   B. aluminum-zinc
    C. copper-arsenic   D. silver

20. H$_2$S in dilute HCl solution is used to precipitate the _____ group.

    A. alkaline earth   B. aluminum-zinc
    C. copper-arsenic   D. silver

21. In analytical work, moisture is *generally* removed from the majority of substances by drying at _____ °C.

    A. 91-95   B. 100-105   C. 121-125   D. 180-185

22. Analytical weights heavier than 1 gram are *usually* composed of

    A. aluminum   B. brass   C. bronze   D. iron

23. Of the following, the one *commonly* used as a laboratory desiccant is

    A. calcium chloride   B. sodium carbonate
    C. sodium chloride   D. potassium nitrate

24. The *policeman* is used in analytical work to

    A. aid in decantation
    B. determine the accuracy of the analytical balance
    C. loosen particles of precipitate
    D. protect a heated crucible

25. The substitution method is *generally* associated with the

    A. calibration of volumetric apparatus
    B. calibration of weights
    C. preparation of chemical indicators
    D. standardization of solutions

KEY (CORRECT ANSWERS)

1.	B	11.	D
2.	A	12.	A
3.	A	13.	C
4.	D	14.	D
5.	B	15.	D
6.	C	16.	B
7.	E	17.	D
8.	D	18.	C
9.	B	19.	D
10.	A	20.	C

21.	B
22.	B
23.	A
24.	C
25.	B

EXAMINATION SECTION
TEST 1

DIRECTIONS: Each question or incomplete statement is followed by several suggested answers or completions. Select the one that BEST answers the question or completes the statement. *PRINT THE LETTER OF THE CORRECT ANSWER IN THE SPACE AT THE RIGHT.*

1. Emery paper is used for

   A. drafting
   B. insulation
   C. moth-proofing cupboards
   D. smoothing wood

2. Natural selection is a theory that explains

   A. Mendelism
   B. sex determination
   C. survival of the fittest
   D. the law of chance

3. An earthquake is recorded by an instrument called a

   A. barograph
   B. seismograph
   C. hygrometer
   D. thermograph

4. A tree whose leaves may be entirely two or three lobed is the

   A. birch   B. elm   C. sassafras   D. willow

5. Echoes are due to

   A. interference
   B. reflection
   C. refraction
   D. resonance

6. The scientist who worked in a field markedly different from that of the others is

   A. William Gorgas
   B. Joseph Henry
   C. Walter Reed
   D. Edward Trudeau

7. Rocky Mountain spotted fever is transmitted by

   A. flies
   B. ticks
   C. mountain goats
   D. mosquitoes

8. In the human body, bacteria are destroyed by

   A. acid in the digestive juices
   B. bone marrow
   C. red blood corpuscles
   D. white blood corpuscles

9. The FAINTEST star that the unaided eye can see is classified as a star of the _____ magnitude.

   A. first   B. second   C. third   D. sixth

10. Of the following, the one which is NOT derived from a fish is

    A. caviar
    B. whale oil
    C. smoked eel
    D. halibut steak

11. The transparent substance through which light travels MOST quickly is 11.____

    A. air B. glass C. lucite D. water

12. On a United States weather map, the barometer readings are given in 12.____

    A. degrees B. millibars
    C. inches D. shaded circles

13. A pilot makes a flight in twelve hours from New York to Los Angeles. 13.____
    If he leaves New York City at 4 A.M. Eastern standard time, he will reach Los Angeles at _____ Pacific standard time.

    A. 1 P.M. B. 2:30 P.M. C. 4 P.M. D. 7 P.M.

14. MOST of the shells found on the beach at Coney Island are the shells of 14.____

    A. clams B. mussels C. scallops D. snails

15. In man, the thorax is separated from the abdomen by a(the) 15.____

    A. diaphragm B. floating rib
    C. layer of fat D. walls of the stomach

16. Of the following foods (average portion), the BEST source of iron is 16.____

    A. white bread B. rye bread
    C. puffed wheat D. oatmeal

17. When toxin-antitoxin is given to a child and it acts FAVORABLY, he is immune to 17.____

    A. diphtheria B. smallpox
    C. rabies D. typhoid

18. The vascular system of the body controls 18.____

    A. elimination of wastes B. circulation of blood
    C. sense of hearing D. respiration

19. The MOST nutritious substitute for meat is 19.____

    A. baked beans B. sweet potato
    C. brown rice D. spaghetti

20. You are called to the gymnasium because of a serious accident to a pupil. 20.____
    Of the following conditions, the one you would treat FIRST while waiting for an ambulance is

    A. severe head injury
    B. unconsciousness
    C. a bad gash on the leg which is spurting blood
    D. a broken leg

21. Overstimulated nervous children are MORE likely than phlegmatic children to have a tendency toward 21.____

    A. chorea B. epilepsy C. hyperopia D. lordosis

22. Of the following foods, the one which contributes MOST to the growth and repair of tissue is   22.____

   A. carrots   B. fish   C. bananas   D. applesauce

23. A pupil is MOST likely suffering from measles if he has an eruption of the skin preceded by   23.____

   A. sick stomach   B. swollen glands
   C. bad cough   D. running nose

24. A study of colds among school children shows that children catch FEWEST colds in school when the   24.____

   A. rooms are kept warm and cozy
   B. pupils have a morning exercise period in the open air
   C. classroom temperature is kept at about 68°
   D. windows of classrooms are kept open to let in much fresh air

25. The cornea of the eye is that part of the eye which   25.____

   A. brings light rays to a focus on the retina
   B. is a muscle for contracting or relaxing the pupil
   C. permits rays of light to enter
   D. is the inner lining of the eyeball

KEY (CORRECT ANSWERS)

1.	D	11.	A
2.	C	12.	C
3.	B	13.	A
4.	C	14.	A
5.	B	15.	A
6.	B	16.	D
7.	B	17.	A
8.	D	18.	B
9.	D	19.	A
10.	B	20.	C

21.	A
22.	B
23.	D
24.	B
25.	A

TEST 2

DIRECTIONS: Each question or incomplete statement is followed by several suggested answers or completions. Select the one that BEST answers the question or completes the statement. *PRINT THE LETTER OF THE CORRECT ANSWER IN THE SPACE AT THE RIGHT.*

1. One of the factors that has markedly influenced the topography of New York City and its environs in RECENT geologic time is 1.____

    A. continental uplift B. exfoliation
    C. glaciation D. vulcanism

2. A unique feature of the hydrogen bomb is that it operates on the principle of 2.____

    A. atomic fission B. atomic synthesis
    C. nuclear energy D. electron emission

3. Silverware exposed to the air turns black because the air contains compounds of 3.____

    A. carbon B. sulfur C. phosphorus D. silicon

4. Fermentation of sugar results in the following products: 4.____

    A. water and ethyl alcohol
    B. water and carbon dioxide
    C. starch and water
    D. ethyl alcohol and carbon dioxide

5. The watt is a unit of electrical 5.____

    A. current B. energy C. power D. pressure

6. New varieties of plants are originated by all of the following methods EXCEPT 6.____

    A. grafting B. selection
    C. hybridizing D. treatment with chemicals

7. The general function of endocrine glands is MOST closely related to that of the _____ system. 7.____

    A. digestive B. nervous
    C. skeletal D. lymphatic

8. The typing of blood is necessary before transfusions are given in order to prevent 8.____

    A. clumping of the red blood cells
    B. destruction of white blood cells
    C. jaundice
    D. sharp changes in blood pressure

9. Two elements obtained from the sea in commercial quantities are 9.____

    A. sulfur and gold B. iodine and aluminum
    C. copper and sodium D. magnesium and bromine

10. Fossils are COMMONLY found in rocks known as 10.____

    A. sedimentary B. archeozoic
    C. metamorphic D. igneous

11. A practical garden aid, useful for destroying weeds in lawns, is

    A. freon B. DDT C. zeolite D. 2,4-D

11.____

12. Chemical fire extinguishers USUALLY put out fires by smothering them with

    A. hydrogen
    C. helium
    B. nitrogen
    D. carbon dioxide

12.____

13. An electromagnetic device for increasing or decreasing voltage is called a(n)

    A. accumulator
    C. resistor
    B. rectifier
    D. transformer

13.____

14. One product of photosynthesis in green plants is

    A. carbon dioxide
    C. nitrogen
    B. oxygen
    D. water

14.____

15. The laws of heredity were FIRST formulated as the result of experiments on the

    A. evening primrose
    C. fruit fly
    B. guinea pig
    D. pea plant

15.____

16. The antibiotic discovered by Waksman is named

    A. streptomycin
    C. chloromycetin
    B. aureomycin
    D. terramycin

16.____

17. When radioactive iodine is injected into the body, it is USUALLY found concentrated in the

    A. adrenals B. pancreas C. thyroid D. pituitary

17.____

18. An important and inexpensive substitute for radium that can be produced in a nuclear reactor is radioactive

    A. barium B. silver C. cobalt D. nickel

18.____

19. Bile helps in the digestion of

    A. carbohydrates
    C. minerals
    B. fats
    D. proteins

19.____

20. Bacteria are USUALLY classified as

    A. plants B. animals C. minerals D. viruses

20.____

21. *Give me a place to stand and a lever long enough and I will move the earth* is a quotation traditionally attributed to

    A. Archimedes
    C. Galileo
    B. Democritus
    D. Newton

21.____

22. All antibiotics are alike in that they

    A. are effective against virus infections
    B. are produced by living organisms
    C. must be administered by injection
    D. have all been synthesized

22.____

23. A native American tree that has become virtually extinct as the result of a blight is the   23.____

    A. black walnut   B. chestnut
    C. elm   D. sweet gum

24. The nucleus of an atom contains the atomic particles   24.____

    A. electrons and protons   B. electrons and neutrons
    C. neutrons and protons   D. positrons and electrons

25. Citrus fruits in the diet prevent   25.____

    A. beriberi   B. pellagra   C. scurvy   D. rickets

KEY (CORRECT ANSWERS)

1. C   11. D
2. B   12. D
3. B   13. D
4. D   14. B
5. C   15. D

6. A   16. A
7. B   17. C
8. A   18. C
9. D   19. B
10. A   20. A

21. A
22. B
23. B
24. C
25. C

TEST 3

DIRECTIONS: Each question or incomplete statement is followed by several suggested answers or completions. Select the one that BEST answers the question or completes the statement. *PRINT THE LETTER OF THE CORRECT ANSWER IN THE SPACE AT THE RIGHT.*

1. When water at 4° C is cooled to 0° C, its

   A. density increases
   B. density remains unchanged
   C. volume increases
   D. volume remains unchanged

   1.____

2. The high temperature necessary for ignition in a diesel engine is produced by

   A. an electric spark   B. friction
   C. combustion   D. compression

   2.____

3. Which one of the following statements about electrical transformers is CORRECT? Step

   A. up transformers increase wattage
   B. down transformers decrease amperage
   C. up transformers increase power
   D. down transformers decrease voltage

   3.____

4. If middle C has a frequency of 256, then the note 2 octaves above middle C has a vibration rate of APPROXIMATELY

   A. 64   B. 85   C. 512   D. 1024

   4.____

5. The trajectory of a bullet shot into space at an angle of 45° with the earth's surface is a portion of a(n)

   A. ellipse   B. parabola   C. circle   D. hyperbola

   5.____

6. Which one of the following scientific principles seems to be MOST clearly contradicted by the Einstein equation $E = MC^2$?

   A. Avogadro's Hypothesis
   B. Universal Law of Gravitation
   C. Newton's 3rd Law
   D. Law of Conservation of Mass

   6.____

7. Of the following, helium nuclei are MOST closely related to _____ rays.

   A. alpha   B. beta   C. gamma   D. cathode

   7.____

8. Implements used by primitive man are often dated by means of radioactive

   A. strontium   B. nitrogen   C. carbon   D. phosphorus

   8.____

9. In ordinary water, the percentage of hydrogen by weight is CLOSEST to which one of the following?

    A. 11% B. 33 1/3% C. 50% D. 66 2/3%

10. Of the following processes, the one which is fundamental in the extraction of metals from their ores is

    A. reduction
    B. polymerization
    C. hydrolysis
    D. crystallization

11. Of the following, the light-sensitive material in a photographic film is USUALLY silver

    A. bromide
    B. oxide
    C. hyposulfite
    D. thiosulfate

12. Of the following groups of scientists, which one contains three men, all of whom did their major work in the same area?

    A. Pasteur, Jenner, Leibnitz
    B. Reed, Newton, Koch
    C. Maxwell, Hertz, Marconi
    D. Armstrong, DeVries, Rutherford

13. The weather NORMALLY associated with the passage of an uncomplicated cold front is characterized by

    A. steady precipitation, slow clearing, and sudden drop in temperature
    B. steady precipitation, rapid clearing, and sudden increase in temperature
    C. showers, rapid clearing, and sudden drop in tempera-ture
    D. showers, slow clearing, and sudden drop in temperature

14. All of the following represent the changing of a sedimentary rock into a metamorphic rock EXCEPT

    A. shale into slate
    B. granite into gneiss
    C. limestone into marble
    D. sandstone into quartzite

15. During which phase of the moon is an eclipse of the sun MOST likely to occur?

    A. New B. Full C. Quarter D. Gibbous

16. Astronomers use the term *magnitude* to denote

    A. size of stars
    B. apparent brightness
    C. telescope range
    D. telescope magnification ratio

17. Which one of the following is NOT an insect?

    A. Praying mantis
    B. Mite
    C. Locust
    D. Cicada

18. The flowers in all of the following are harbingers of spring in the eastern United States EXCEPT

    A. forsythia B. crocus C. aster D. red maple

19. When two pea plants, both of which are hybrid with respect to tallness and shortness (tall is dominant), are crossed, the offspring will, assuming pure operation of the laws of probability, divide themselves into a tall to short ratio of

    A. 4:1   B. 3:1   C. 2:1   D. 1:1

19.____

20. A fruit is a ripened

    A. ovary   B. ovule   C. flower   D. embryo

20.____

21. Cortisone is produced by the

    A. adrenals   B. islands of Langerhans
    C. pituitary   D. liver

21.____

22. Which one of the following choices is MOST like root hairs in function?

    A. Cilia   B. Villi   C. Arteries D. Stomates

22.____

23. In the usual system of atomic and molecular weights, the oxygen molecule has a weight of

    A. 1   B. 12   C. 16   D. 32

23.____

24. The atomic number of an element is ALWAYS equal to

    A. half its atomic weight
    B. the number of protons and neutrons in the nucleus
    C. the electrical charge on the nucleus
    D. the number of neutrons in the nucleus

24.____

25. When a diamond is burned, which one of the following occurs? The

    A. resulting ash weighs more than the original diamond
    B. gas CO_2 is formed
    C. extremely hard substance carborundum is formed
    D. gas ammonia is formed

25.____

KEY (CORRECT ANSWERS)

1. C
2. D
3. D
4. D
5. B

6. D
7. A
8. C
9. A
10. A

11. A
12. C
13. C
14. B
15. A

16. B
17. B
18. C
19. B
20. A

21. A
22. B
23. D
24. C
25. B

TEST 4

DIRECTIONS: Each question or incomplete statement is followed by several suggested answers or completions. Select the one that BEST answers the question or completes the statement. *PRINT THE LETTER OF THE CORRECT ANSWER IN THE SPACE AT THE RIGHT.*

1. Globulins are   1.____

   A. digestive enzymes B. hormones
   C. dietary essentials D. blood proteins

2. To combat the erosion of cultivable soil, farmers are being advised to employ   2.____

   A. irrigation B. rotation of crops
   C. chemical fertilizers D. contour plowing

3. Of the following, the one that is a hormone is   3.____

   A. ascorbic acid B. adrenalin
   C. penicillin D. pepsin

4. Which one of the following is based on a principle different from that of the others?   4.____

   A. Exhaust pump B. Pneumatic drill
   C. Air brake D. Tire gauge

5. Of the following, the statement which is NOT true is that the sun   5.____

   A. is a star
   B. is a stationary body
   C. varies in its distance from the earth
   D. rotates on its axis

6. Reptiles are   6.____

   A. amphibious
   B. vertebrates
   C. the most highly developed invertebrates
   D. quadrupeds

7. The quasispherical shape of a dew drop is explained by   7.____

   A. air pressure B. gravity
   C. streamlining D. surface tension

8. Fire extinguishers should be inspected and recharged   8.____

   A. only after use B. annually
   C. monthly D. every five years

9. Experiments are now in progress to ascertain whether the development of good teeth is dependent on the inclusion in the diet of   9.____

   A. iodine B. bromine C. fluorine D. iron

10. The greater the difference in temperature between the wet and dry bulbs of a hygrometer, the LOWER is the

   A. atmosphere pressure
   B. air velocity
   C. relative humidity
   D. salinity of the water used

10._____

11. An animal group that now contains only a single species is

   A. the camel
   B. the mosquito
   C. man
   D. the monkey

11._____

12. The term *colloids* is used in contradistinction to

   A. crystalline substances
   B. organic compounds
   C. plastics
   D. catalysts

12._____

13. A substance which is NOT used as a source of atomic energy is

   A. plutonium   B. thorium   C. uranium   D. vanadium

13._____

14. A nutcracker is FUNDAMENTALLY a(n)

   A. inclined plane
   B. screw
   C. lever
   D. wedge

14._____

15. A kilowatt-hour is a unit of electrical

   A. resistance
   B. voltage
   C. time
   D. energy

15._____

16. Hydrogen in a dirigible balloon becomes contaminated by the process of

   A. crystallization
   B. diffusion
   C. gravitation
   D. oxidation

16._____

17. The liquid from which the cells of our body obtain nourishment is

   A. cell sap
   B. lymph
   C. hemoglobin
   D. gastric juice

17._____

18. When atmospheric *highs* and *lows* are near one another, which one of the following results is MOST likely to occur?

   A. Dead calm
   B. Strong winds
   C. Thunderstorms
   D. Cold wave

18._____

19. In the helicopter, lift is provided by the

   A. ailerons   B. fuselage   C. rotors   D. rudders

19._____

20. Of the following, the BEST definition of a chemical formula is a

   A. device for indicating the physical and chemical properties of a substance
   B. set of symbols which shows the number and kind of atoms in a compound
   C. abbreviated chemical equation
   D. symbol indicating the kind of elements in a mixture

20._____

21. An object falling through space reaches a terminal velocity. Which one of the following statements gives the BEST explanation of this phenomenon?
    The

    A. air resistance counterbalances the force of gravity
    B. force of gravity decreases with the time of fall
    C. speed of an object cannot increase indefinitely
    D. value of gravity decreases to zero at the earth's surface

22. Cooking in an open vessel is MOST destructive to vitamin

    A. A   B. B   C. C   D. D

23. The disease whose cause is MOST distinctly different from that of the others is

    A. botulism   B. cretinism
    C. diabetes   D. hyperthyroidism

24. The man who FIRST described the species native to the Galapagos Islands was

    A. Chapman   B. Lamarck   C. Huxley   D. Darwin

25. The effect produced when two tuning forks of slightly different frequency are sounded together is called

    A. beats   B. overtones
    C. resonances   D. sympathetic vibration

KEY (CORRECT ANSWERS)

1. D		11. C	
2. D		12. A	
3. B		13. D	
4. A		14. C	
5. B		15. D	
6. B		16. B	
7. D		17. B	
8. B		18. B	
9. C		19. C	
10. C		20. B	

21. A
22. C
23. A
24. D
25. A

TEST 5

DIRECTIONS: Each question or incomplete statement is followed by several suggested answers or completions. Select the one that BEST answers the question or completes the statement. *PRINT THE LETTER OF THE CORRECT ANSWER IN THE SPACE AT THE RIGHT.*

1. The formula for dry ice is

   A. CO_2 B. H_2O C. (SiO_2) D. SO_2

2. Which one of the following offers the BEST experimental support for the statement that the molecules of a gas are relatively far apart?

   A. Gases are highly compressible.
   B. Gases diffuse into one another.
   C. Gas molecules show Brownian movement.
   D. Gas molecules are exceedingly small.

3. An electro-magnetic effect makes possible

   A. electric doorbells   B. incandescent light bulbs
   C. the plating of silverware D. radiant heaters

4. The fact that strips of metal expand when heated is used as the construction principle of the

   A. aneroid barometer   B. clinical thermometer
   C. micrometer calipers D. thermostat

5. A knot in a board is caused by

   A. abnormal growth
   B. the activity of infesting insects
   C. the growth of a branch
   D. the rupture of the bark

6. The substance with the HIGHEST boiling point is

   A. ether   B. alcohol
   C. Rose's metal D. mercury

7. Rains are caused by

   A. cold fronts being pushed upward
   B. cold fronts being pushed downward
   C. warm fronts rising over cold fronts
   D. warm fronts going under cold fronts

8. Lines on a daily weather map that connect places with the same atmospheric pressure are called

   A. isotherms B. isobars
   C. barographs D. thermographs

9. The constellation that can be seen at any time of the year in New York is 9.____

   A. Cassiopeia B. Orion
   C. Andromeda   D. Leo

10. If the earth's axis were perpendicular to the plane of its orbit, the 10.____

    A. seasonal changes in temperature would be greater
    B. seasonal changes in temperature would be less
    C. days and nights would vary more widely in length during different seasons
    D. days and nights would vary less during the different seasons

11. The statement that is NOT true about an atomic reactor is that the 11.____

    A. fission process in the reactor leaves no waste
    B. reactor is part of an atomic power plant
    C. atomic reactor is a kind of furnace for producing heat
    D. atomic reactor must contain sufficient fissionable material to sustain a chain reaction

12. To make food, green plants must use all of the following EXCEPT 12.____

    A. sunlight
    B. carbon dioxide and moisture
    C. oxygen
    D. chlorophyll

13. Birds that catch insects in flight have beaks that are 13.____

    A. pointed and sharp   B. long and thick
    C. short and thick   D. short and wide

14. Two identical books are placed at one end of a lever and ten of the same books at the other end. 14.____
    To make the two books balance the ten books, the fulcrum MUST be

    A. at the center of the lever
    B. between the center of the lever and the two books
    C. between the center of the lever and the ten books
    D. directly under the two books

15. A fireplace warms people that are near it because heat 15.____

    A. sets up convection currents
    B. diffuses
    C. expands air
    D. is radiated

16. It does not get dark immediately after the sun sets because 16.____

    A. some light is absorbed by the earth
    B. light is reflected from dust in the atmosphere
    C. light is reflected from parts of the earth on which the sun is shining
    D. light rays are bent by the clouds

17. When sugar is lodged in the teeth, cavities enlarge rapidly because bacteria uses it to

    A. form acids which dissolve calcium salts
    B. form toxins which soften teeth
    C. assimilate calcium salts
    D. form enzymes which dissolve calcium salts

17.____

18. Irregular curvature of the eye's cornea causes

    A. astigmatism   B. myopia
    C. hyperopia   D. strabismus

18.____

19. The alloy used in fuses MUST

    A. contain copper
    B. melt at high temperature
    C. melt at low temperature
    D. have high electrical resistance

19.____

20. Rocks are changed to soil by

    A. fission   B. pressure
    C. weathering   D. erosion

20.____

21. The part of the brain that controls the coordination of muscles is the

    A. cerebrum   B. cerebellum
    C. medulla oblongata   D. occipital lobe

21.____

22. A liquid in which the molecules of one substance are uniformly distributed among the molecules of another substance is a

    A. suspension   B. solution
    C. solute   D. solvent

22.____

23. A basal metabolism test provides information concerning the body's

    A. circulatory system   B. speed of digestion
    C. nervous system   D. rate of oxidation

23.____

24. Valves in wind musical instruments

    A. control the loudness of the sound produced
    B. keep air columns from vibrating
    C. make air columns vibrate
    D. change the length of the air columns

24.____

25. An electric motor rotates because the current passing through the coils produces

    A. magnetism   B. radioactivity
    C. chemical changes   D. heat

25.____

KEY (CORRECT ANSWERS)

1. A
2. A
3. A
4. D
5. C

6. D
7. C
8. B
9. A
10. B

11. A
12. C
13. D
14. C
15. D

16. B
17. A
18. A
19. C
20. C

21. B
22. B
23. D
24. D
25. A

READING COMPREHENSION
UNDERSTANDING AND INTERPRETING WRITTEN MATERIAL
EXAMINATION SECTION
TEST 1

DIRECTIONS: Each question or incomplete statement is followed by several suggested answers or completions. Select the one that BEST answers the question or completes the statement. *PRINT THE LETTER OF THE CORRECT ANSWER IN THE SPACE AT THE RIGHT.*

Questions 1-8.

DIRECTIONS: Questions 1 through 8, inclusive, are to be answered in accordance with the following information.

In his 2017 annual report to the Mayor, the Public Works Commissioner stated that the city's basic water pollution control program begun in 1981 and costing $425 million so far would be completed in five or six years at a cost of $275 million more. However, he said, the city must spend an additional $175 million more on its marginal pollution control program to protect present and proposed beaches. Under the basic program, the city will have eliminated the last major discharges of raw sewage into the harbor. Over 800 million gallons, two-thirds of the city's spent water each day, is now treated at 12 plants, to which six new plants will be added, enabling the city to treat the estimated 1.8 billion gallons that will be discharged daily in 2050. The department had about $200 million worth of municipal construction under way in 2017, and completed $85.5 millions' worth.

1. According to the above, the city will add _____ new plants.
   A. 18   B. 12   C. 6   D. 4

2. The amount of municipal construction under way in 2017 was _____ million.
   A. $85.5   B. $175   C. $200   D. $425

3. It is estimated that in 2050 the city will treat daily _____ gallons.
   A. 700 million   B. 800 million   C. 900 million   D. 1.8 billion

4. According to the above article, the total cost of the water pollution program begun in 1981 will be _____ million.
   A. $275   B. $425   C. $700   D. $815

5. According to the above article, to protect present and proposed beaches, the city must spend an additional _____ million.
   A. $175   B. $275   C. $425   D. $450

6. The above article concerns the statements of the Commissioner of Public Works in his _____ annual report to the Mayor.
   A. 1981   B. 2050   C. 2017   D. 2018

7. The word *discharged* as used in the above article means MOST NEARLY

   A. emitted   B. erased   C. refuted   D. repelled

8. The word *pollution* as used in the above article means MOST NEARLY

   A. condensation
   C. contamination
   B. purification
   D. distillation

Questions 9-15.

DIRECTIONS: Questions 9 through 15, inclusive, are to be answered in accordance with the following information.

At sea level the atmosphere can exert a pressure of 14.7 pounds per square inch. This pressure is capable of sustaining a column of water having a height equal to 14.7 pounds multiplied by 2.304 (the height of water in feet which will exert one pound per square inch pressure). No pump built can produce a perfect vacuum. The atmospheric pressure exerting its force on the surface of the water from which suction is being taken forces the water up through the suction to the pump. From this, it is evident that the maximum height which a water pump of this type can lift water is determined ultimately by the atmospheric pressure. The tightness of the pump and its ability to create a vacuum also have a bearing.

9. The meaning of the word *vacuum* as used in the above article is a

   A. space entirely devoid of matter
   B. sealed tube filled with gas
   C. bottle-shaped vessel with a double wall
   D. cleaning device

10. With reference to the above article, if a pump could produce a perfect vacuum, the MAXIMUM height, in feet, that it could lift water at sea level is MOST NEARLY

    A. 33.9   B. 29.4   C. 23.3   D. 14.7

11. With reference to the above article, a column of water having a height of 4.6 feet at sea level will exert a pressure of MOST NEARLY _____ pounds per square inch.

    A. 3   B. 2   C. 1   D. $\frac{1}{2}$

12. The word *atmosphere* as used in the above article means

    A. the pull of gravity
    B. perfect vacuum
    C. the whole mass of air surrounding the earth
    D. the weight of water at sea level

13. The word *bearing* as used in the above article means MOST NEARLY

    A. direction
    C. divergence
    B. connection
    D. convergence

14. The word *evident* as used in the above article means MOST NEARLY 14.____

    A. disconcerting B. obscure
    C. equivocal D. manifest

15. The word *maximum* as used in the above article means MOST NEARLY 15.____

    A. best B. median C. adjacent D. greatest

Questions 16-19.

DIRECTIONS: Questions 16 through 19, inclusive, are to be answered in accordance with the following paragraph.

One of the categories of nuisance is a chemical one and relates to the dissolved oxygen of the watercourse. The presence in sewage and industrial wastes of materials capable of undergoing biochemical oxidation and resulting in reduction of oxygen in the watercourse leads to a partial or complete depletion of this oxygen. This, in turn, leads to the subsequent production of malodorous products of decomposition, to the destruction of aquatic plant life and major fish life, and to conditions offensive to sight and smell.

16. The word *malodorous* as used in the above paragraph means MOST NEARLY 16.____

    A. fragrant B. fetid C. wholesome D. redolent

17. From the above paragraph, because of pollution the amount of dissolved oxygen in the waterways is 17.____

    A. released B. multiplied
    C. lessened D. saturated

18. The word *categories* as used in the above paragraph means MOST NEARLY 18.____

    A. divisions B. clubs C. symbols D. products

19. The word *offensive* as used in the above paragraph means MOST NEARLY 19.____

    A. pliable B. complaint
    C. deferential D. disagreeable

Questions 20-22.

DIRECTIONS: Questions 20 through 22, inclusive, are to be answered in accordance with the following paragraph.

Thermostats should be tested in hot water for proper opening. A bucket should be filled with sufficient water to cover the thermostat and fitted with a thermometer suspended in the water so that the sensitive bulb portion does not rest directly on the bucket. The water is then heated on a stove. As the temperature of the water passes the 160-165° range, the thermostat should start to open and should be completely opened when the temperature has risen to 185-190°. Lifting the thermostat into the air should cause a pronounced closing action, and the unit should be closed entirely within a short time.

20. The thermostat described above is a device which opens and closes with changes in the   20.____

    A. position
    B. pressure
    C. temperature
    D. surroundings

21. According to the above paragraph, the closing action of the thermostat should be tested by   21.____

    A. working the thermostat back and forth
    B. permitting the water to cool gradually
    C. adding cold water to the bucket
    D. removing the thermostat from the bucket

22. The bulb of the thermometer should NOT rest directly on the bucket because   22.____

    A. the bucket gets hotter than the water
    B. the thermometer might be damaged in that position
    C. it is difficult to read the thermometer in that position
    D. the thermometer might interfere with operation of the thermostat

Questions 23-25.

DIRECTIONS: Questions 23 through 25, inclusive, are to be answered in accordance with information given in the paragraph below.

All idle pumps should be turned daily by hand and should be run under power at least once a week. Whenever repairs are made on a pump, a record should be kept so that it will be possible to judge the success with which the pump is performing its functions. If a pump fails to deliver liquid, there may be an obstruction in the suction line, the pump's parts may be badly worn, or the packing defective.

23. According to the above paragraph, pumps   23.____

    A. in use should be turned by hand every day
    B. which are not in use should be run under power every day
    C. which are in daily use should be run under power several times a week
    D. which are not in use should be turned by hand every day

24. According to the above paragraph, the reason for keeping records of repairs made on pumps is to   24.____

    A. make certain that proper maintenance is being performed
    B. discover who is responsible for improper repairs
    C. rate the performance of the pumps
    D. know when to replace worn parts

25. The one of the following causes of pump failure which is NOT mentioned in the above paragraph is   25.____

    A. excessive suction lift
    B. clogged lines
    C. bad packing
    D. worn parts

KEY (CORRECT ANSWERS)

1.	C		11.	B
2.	C		12.	C
3.	D		13.	B
4.	C		14.	D
5.	A		15.	D
6.	C		16.	B
7.	A		17.	C
8.	C		18.	A
9.	A		19.	D
10.	A		20.	C

21. D
22. A
23. D
24. C
25. A

TEST 2

DIRECTIONS: Each question or incomplete statement is followed by several suggested answers or completions. Select the one that BEST answers the question or completes the statement. *PRINT THE LETTER OF THE CORRECT ANSWER IN THE SPACE AT THE RIGHT.*

Questions 1-2.

DIRECTIONS: Questions 1 and 2 are to be answered in accordance with the information given in the following paragraph.

    A sludge lagoon is an excavated area in which digested sludge is desired. Lagoon depths vary from six to eight feet. There are no established criteria for the required capacity of a lagoon. The sludge moisture content is reduced by evaporation and drainage. Volume reduction is slow, especially in cold and rainy weather. Weather and soil conditions affect concentration. The drying period ranges from a period of several months to several years. After the sludge drying period has ended, a bulldozer or tractor can be used to remove the sludge. The dried sludge can be used for fill of low ground. A filled dried lagoon can be developed into a lawn. Lagoons can be used for emergency storage when the sludge beds are full. Lagoons are popular because they are inexpensive to build and operate. They have a disadvantage of being unsightly. A hazard to lagoon operation is the possibility of draining partly digested sludge to the lagoon that creates a fly and odor nuisance.

1. In accordance with the given paragraph, sludge lagoons have the disadvantage of being   1.____

    A. unsightly   B. too deep
    C. concentrated   D. wet

2. In accordance with the given paragraph, moisture content is reduced by   2.____

    A. digestion   B. evaporation
    C. oxidation   D. removal

Questions 3-5.

DIRECTIONS: Questions 3 through 5, inclusive, should be answered in accordance with the following paragraph.

    Sharpening a twist drill by hand is a skill that is mastered only after much practice and careful attention to the details. Therefore, whenever possible, use a tool grinder in which the drills can be properly positioned, clamped in place, and set with precision for the various angles. This machine grinding will enable you to sharpen the drills accurately. As a result, they will last longer and will produce more accurate holes.

3. According to the above paragraph, one reason for sharpening drills accurately is that the drills   3.____

    A. can then be used in a hand drill as well as a drill press
    B. will last longer
    C. can then be used by unskilled persons
    D. cost less

4. According to the above paragraph,

   A. it is easier to sharpen a drill by machine than by hand
   B. drills cannot be sharpened by hand
   C. only a skilled mechanic can learn to sharpen a drill by hand
   D. a good mechanic will learn to sharpen drills by hand

5. As used in the above paragraph, the word *precision* means MOST NEARLY

   A. accuracy   B. ease   C. rigidity   D. speed

Questions 6-9.

DIRECTIONS: Questions 6 through 9, inclusive, should be answered in accordance with the following paragraph.

Centrifugal pumps have relatively fewer moving parts than reciprocating pumps, and no valves. While reciprocating pumps when new are usually more efficient than centrifugal pumps, the latter retain their efficiency longer. Most rotary pumps are also without valves, but they have closely meshing parts between which high pressures may be set up after they begin to wear. In general, centrifugal pumps can be made much smaller than reciprocating pumps giving the same result. There is an exception in that positive displacement pumps delivering small volumes at high heads are smaller than equivalent centrifugal pumps. Centrifugal pumps cost less when first purchased than other comparable pumps. The original outlay may be as little as one-third or one-half that of a reciprocating pump suitable for the same purpose.

6. The type of pump NOT mentioned in the above paragraph is the _____ type.

   A. rotary   B. propeller
   C. reciprocating   D. centrifugal

7. According to the above paragraph, the type of pump that sometimes has valves and sometimes does NOT is the

   A. rotary   B. propeller
   C. reciprocating   D. centrifugal

8. According to the above paragraph, centrifugal pumps are

   A. *always* smaller than reciprocating pumps
   B. *smaller* than reciprocating pumps only when designed to deliver small quantities at low pressures
   C. *larger* than reciprocating pumps only when designed to deliver small quantities at high pressures
   D. *larger* than reciprocating pumps only when designed to deliver large quantities at low pressures

9. The advantage of centrifugal pumps that is NOT mentioned in the above paragraph is that

   A. the centrifugal pump retains its efficiency longer
   B. it is impossible to create an excessive pressure when using a centrifugal pump

C. there are fewer parts to wear out in a centrifugal pump
D. the centrifugal pump is cheaper

Questions 10-12.

DIRECTIONS: Questions 10 through 12, inclusive, should be answered in accordance with the following paragraph.

Gaskets made of relatively soft materials are placed between the meeting surfaces of hydraulic fittings in order to increase the tightness of the seal. They should be composed of materials that will not be affected by the liquid to be enclosed, nor by the conditions under which the system operates, including maximum pressure and temperature. They should be able to maintain the amount of clearance required between meeting surfaces. One of the materials most widely used in making gaskets is neoprene. Since neoprene is flexible, it is often used in sheet form at points where a gasket must expand enough to allow air to accumulate, as with cover plates on supply tanks. Over a period of time, oil tends to deteriorate the material used in making neoprene gaskets. The condition of the gasket must, therefore, be checked whenever the unit is disassembled. Since neoprene gasket material is soft and flexible, it easily becomes misshapen, scratched or torn. Great care is therefore necessary in handling neoprene. Shellac, gasket sealing compounds or *pipe dope* should never be used with sheet neoprene, unless absolutely necessary for satisfactory installation.

10. Of the following, the one that is NOT mentioned in the above paragraph as a requirement for a good gasket material is that the material must be

    A. cheap
    B. unaffected by heat developed in a system
    C. relatively soft
    D. capable of maintaining required clearances

11. According to the above paragraph, neoprene will be affected by

    A. air   B. temperature   C. pressure   D. oil

12. According to the above paragraph, care is necessary in handling neoprene because

    A. its condition must be checked frequently
    B. it tears easily
    C. pipe dope should not be used
    D. it is difficult to use

Questions 13-15.

DIRECTIONS: Questions 13 through 15, inclusive, are to be answered in accordance with the information given in the paragraph below.

Some gases which may be inhaled have an irritant effect on the respiratory tract. Among them are ammonia fumes, hydrogen sulfide, nitrous fumes, and phosgene. Persons who have been exposed to irritant gases must lie down at once and keep absolutely quiet until the dotor arrives. The action of some of these gases may be delayed, and at first the victim may show few or no symptoms.

13. According to the above paragraph, the part of the body that is MOST affected by irritant gases is the

    A. heart   B. lungs   C. skin   D. nerves

14. According to the above paragraph, a person who has inhaled an irritant gas should be

    A. given artificial respiration
    B. made to rest
    C. wrapped in blankets
    D. made to breathe smelling salts

15. A person is believed to have come in contact with an irritant gas but he does not become sick immediately.
    According to the above paragraph, we may conclude that the person

    A. did not really come in contact with the gas
    B. will become sick later
    C. came in contact with a small amount of gas
    D. may possibly become sick later

Questions 16-22.

DIRECTIONS: Questions 16 through 22, inclusive, are to be answered in accordance with the following paragraph.

At 2:30 P.M. on Monday, October 25, Mr. Paul Jones, a newly appointed sewage treatment worker, started on a routine inspectional tour of the settling tanks and other sewage treatment works installations of the plant to which he was assigned. At 2:33 P.M., Mr. Jones discovered a co-worker, Mr. James P. Brown, lying unconscious on the ground. Mr. Jones quickly reported the facts to his immediate superior, Mr. Jack Rota, who immediately telephoned for an ambulance. Mr. Rota then rushed to the site and placed a heavy woolen blanket over the victim. Mr. Brown was taken to the Ave. H hospital by an ambulance driven by Mr. Dave Smith, which arrived at the sewage disposal plant at 3:02 P.M. Patrolman Robert Daly, badge number 12520, had arrived before the ambulance and recorded all the details of the incident, including the statements of Mr. Jones, Mr. Rota, and Mr. Nick Nespola, a Stationary Engineer (Electric), who stated that he saw the victim when he fell to the ground.

16. The time which elapsed between the start of the sewage treatment worker's routine inspection and the arrival of the ambulance was MOST NEARLY _____ minutes.

    A. 3   B. 28   C. 29   D. 32

17. The name of the sewage treatment worker's immediate superior was

    A. James P. Brown   B. Jack Rota
    C. Paul Jones   D. Robert Daly

18. The name of the patrolman was

    A. James P. Brown   B. Jack Rota
    C. Paul Jones   D. Robert Daly

19. Referring to the above, the incident occurred on   19._____

    A. Monday, Oct. 25   B. Monday, Oct. 26
    C. Tuesday, Oct. 25   D. Tuesday, Oct. 26

20. The victim was found at exactly   20._____

    A. 2:30 A.M.   B. 2:33 P.M.   C. 2:33 A.M.   D. 2:30 P.M.

21. The sewage treatment worker's name was   21._____

    A. James P. Brown   B. Jack Rota
    C. Paul Jones   D. Dave Smith

22. The man named Nick Nespola was the   22._____

    A. Stationary Engineer (Electric)
    B. patrolman
    C. victim
    D. ambulance driver

Questions 23-25.

DIRECTIONS: Questions 23 through 25, inclusive, are to be answered in accordance with the information given in the paragraph below.

The bearings of all electrical equipment should be subjected to careful inspection at scheduled periodic intervals in order to secure maximum life. The newer type of sleeve bearings requires very little attention since the oil does not become contaminated and oil leakage is negligible. Maintenance of the correct oil level is frequently the only upkeep required for years of service with this type of bearing.

23. According to the above paragraph, the MAIN reason for making periodic inspections of electrical equipment is to   23._____

    A. reduce waste of lubricants
    B. prevent injury to operators
    C. make equipment last longer
    D. keep operators *on their toes*

24. According to the above paragraph, the bearings of electrical equipment should be inspected   24._____

    A. whenever the equipment isn't working properly
    B. whenever there is time for inspections
    C. at least once a year
    D. at regular times

25. According to the above paragraph, when using newer type of sleeve bearings,   25._____

    A. oil leakage is slight
    B. the oil level should be checked every few years
    C. oil leakage is due to carelessness
    D. oil soon becomes dirty

KEY (CORRECT ANSWERS)

1.	A	11.	D
2.	B	12.	B
3.	B	13.	B
4.	A	14.	B
5.	A	15.	D
6.	B	16.	D
7.	A	17.	B
8.	C	18.	D
9.	B	19.	A
10.	A	20.	B

21. C
22. A
23. C
24. D
25. A

TEST 3

DIRECTIONS: Each question or incomplete statement is followed by several suggested answers or completions. Select the one that BEST answers the question or completes the statement. *PRINT THE LETTER OF THE CORRECT ANSWER IN THE SPACE AT THE RIGHT.*

Questions 1-2.

DIRECTIONS: Questions 1 and 2 are to be answered on the basis of the paragraph below.

    When summers are hot and dry, much water will be used for watering lawns. Domestic use will be further increased by more bathing, while public use will be affected by much street sprinkling and use in parks and recreation fields for watering grass and for ornamental fountains. Variations in the weather may cause variations in water consumption. A succession of showers in the summer could significantly reduce water consumption. High temperatures may also lead to high water use for air conditioning purposes. On the other hand, in cold weather water may be wasted at the faucets to prevent freezing of pipes, thereby greatly increasing consumption.

1. According to the above passage, water consumption

    A. will not be affected by the weather to any appreciable extent
    B. will always increase in the warm weather and decrease in cold weather
    C. will increase in cold weather and decrease in warm weather
    D. may increase because of high or low temperatures

1.____

2. The MAIN subject of the above passage is

    A. climatic conditions affecting water consumption
    B. water consumption in arid regions
    C. conservation of water
    D. weather variations

2.____

Questions 3-4.

DIRECTIONS: Questions 3 and 4 are to be answered on the basis of the paragraph below.

    The efficiency of the water works management will affect con-sumption by decreasing loss and waste. Leaks in the water mains and services and unauthorized use of water can be kept to a minimum by surveys. A water supply that is both safe and attractive in quality will be used to a greater extent than one of poor quality. In this connection, it should be recognized that improvement of the quality of water supply will probably be followed by an increase in consumption. Increasing the pressure will have a similar effect. Changing the rates charged for water will also affect consumption. A study found that consumption decreases about five percent for each ten percent increase in water rates. Similarly, water consumption increases when the water rates are decreasing.

3. According to the above passage, an increase in the quality of water would MOST LIKELY

    A. cause an increase in water consumption
    B. decrease water consumption by about 10%

3.____

102

C. cause a decrease in water consumption
D. have no effect on water consumption

4. According to the above passage, a ten percent decrease in water rates would MOST LIKELY result in a _____ in the water consumption.

   A. five percent decrease
   B. five percent increase
   C. ten percent decrease
   D. ten percent increase

4._____

Questions 5-6.

DIRECTIONS: Questions 5 and 6 are to be answered on the basis of the paragraph below.

While the average domestic use of water may be expected to be about 35 gallons per person daily, wide variations are found. These are largely dependent upon the economic status of the consumers and will differ greatly in various sections of the city. In the high value residential districts of a city or in a suburban community of similar type population, the water consumption per person will be high. In apartment houses, which may be considered as representing the maximum domestic demand to be expected, the average consumption should be about 60 gallons per person. In an area of high value single residences, even higher consumption may be expected since to the ordinary domestic demand there will be added amount for watering lawns. The slum districts of large cities will show a consumption per person of about 20 gallons daily. The lowest figures of all will be found in low value districts where sewerage is not available and where perhaps a single faucet serves one or several households.

5. According to the above passage, domestic water consumption per person

   A. would probably be lowest for persons in an area of high value single residences
   B. would probably be lowest for persons in an apartment house
   C. would probably be lowest for persons in a slum area
   D. does not depend at all upon area or income

5._____

6. According to the above passage, the water consumption in apartment houses as compared to slum houses is about _____ times as much.

   A. $1\frac{1}{2}$
   B. 2
   C. $2\frac{1}{2}$
   D. 3

6._____

Questions 7-9.

DIRECTIONS: Questions 7 through 9 are to be answered in accordance with the paragraph below.

A connection for commercial purposes may be made from a metered fire or sprinkler line of 4 inches or larger in diameter, provided a meter is installed on the commercial branch line. Such connection shall be taken from the inlet side of the fire meter control valve, and the method of connection shall be subject to the approval of the department. On a 4-inch fire line, the connection shall not exceed inches in diameter. On a fire line 6 inches or larger in diameter, the size of the connection shall not exceed 2 inches. Fire lines shall not be cross-connected with any system of piping within the building.

7. According to the above paragraph, a connection for commercial purposes may be made to a metered sprinkler line provided that the diameter of the sprinkler line is AT LEAST

   A. $1\frac{1}{2}$" B. 2" C. 4" D. 6"

7.____

8. According to the above paragraph, the connection for commercial purposes is taken from the

   A. inlet side of the main control valve
   B. outlet side of the wet connection
   C. inlet side of the fire meter control valve
   D. outlet side of the Siamese

8.____

9. According to the above paragraph, the MAXIMUM size permitted for the connection for commercial purposes depends on the

   A. location of the fire meter valve
   B. use to which the commercial line is to be put
   C. method of connection to the sprinkler line
   D. size of the sprinkler line

9.____

Questions 10-11.

DIRECTIONS: Questions 10 and 11 are to be answered in accordance with the paragraph below.

Meters shall be set or reset so that they may be easily examined and read. In all premises where the supply of water is to be fully metered, the meter shall be set within three feet of the building or vault wall at. point of entry of service pipe. The service pipe between meter control valve and meter shall be kept exposed. When a building is situated back of the building line or conditions exist in a building that prevent the setting of the meter at a point of entry, meter may be set outside of the building in a proper watertight and frost-proof pit or meter box, or at another location approved by the Deputy Commissioner, Assistant to Commissioner, or the Chief Inspector.

10. According to the above paragraph, a meter should be set

    A. at a point in the building convenient to the owner
    B. within 3 feet of the building wall
    C. in back of the building
    D. where the district inspector thinks is best

10.____

11. According to the above paragraph, one of the conditions imposed when a meter is permitted to be installed outside of a building is that the meter must be installed

    A. between the service pipe and the meter control valve
    B. within 3 feet of the point of entry of the service pipe
    C. in a watertight enclosure
    D. above ground in a frost-proof box

11.____

Questions 12-15.

DIRECTIONS: Questions 12 through 15 are to be answered in accordance with the paragraphs below.

No individual or collective air conditioning system installed on any premises for a single consumer shall be permitted to waste annually more than the equivalent of a continuous flow of five gallons of city water per minute.

All individual or collective air conditioning systems installed on any premises for a single consumer using city water annually in excess of the equivalent of five gallons per minute shall be equipped with a water conserving device such as economizer, evaporative condenser, water cooling tower, or other similar apparatus, which device shall not consume for makeup purposes in excess of 15% of the consumption that would normally be used without such device.

Any individual or collective group of such units installed on any premises for a single consumer with a rated capacity of 25 tons or more, or water consumption of 50 gallons or more per minute, shall be equipped, where required by the department, with a water meter to separately register the consumption of such unit or groups of units.

This rule shall also apply to all air conditioning equipment now in service.

12. The rules described in the above paragraphs apply

    A. *only* to new installations of air conditioning equipment
    B. *only* to air conditioning systems which waste more than 5 gallons of city water per minute
    C. *only* to new installations of air conditioning equipment which waste more than 5 gallons of city water per minute
    D. to all air conditioning systems, whether existing ones or new installations

13. According to the above paragraphs, one of the acceptable methods of reducing wasting of water in an air conditioning system is by means of a

    A. cooling tower   B. water meter
    C. check valve   D. collective system

14. According to the above paragraphs, the department may require that an air conditioning system have a separate water meter when the system

    A. wastes more than 5 gallons of city water per minute
    B. uses more than 15% make-up water
    C. is equipped with an economizer
    D. has a rated capacity of 25 tons or more

15. According to the above paragraphs, the MAXIMUM quantity of make-up water permitted where an air conditioning system uses 50 gallons of water per minute is _____ gallons/minute.

    A. 7   B. $7\frac{1}{2}$ C. 8   D. $8\frac{1}{2}$

Questions 16-17.

DIRECTIONS: Questions 16 and 17 are to be answered in accordance with the paragraph below.

Where flushometers, suction tanks, other fixtures or piping are equipped with quick closing valves and are supplied by direct street pressure in excess of 70 pounds, an air chamber of an approved type shall be installed within two feet of the house control valve or meter in the service near the point of entry. Where water hammer conditions exist in any installation, regardless of the pressure obtaining, an air chamber of an approved type shall be installed where and as directed by the Chief Inspector or Engineer.

16. According to the above paragraph, air chambers are required when or wherever

   A. there are flushometers
   B. piping is supplied at a direct street pressure in excess of 70 lbs. per sq. in.
   C. a quick closing valve is used
   D. water hammer can occur in any piping

17. According to the above paragraph, air chambers should be installed

   A. within two feet of the house control valve or meter
   B. in a water system regardless of operating pressure
   C. on the fixture side of the quick closing valve
   D. on the suction side of the service meter

Questions 18-23.

DIRECTIONS: Questions 18 through 23 are to be answered in accordance with the paragraph below.

The acceptor's responsibility—The purpose of commercial standards is to establish for specific commodities, nationally *recognized* grades or consumer *criteria* and the benefits therefrom will be measurable in direct proportion to their general recognition and actual use. Instances will occur when it may be necessary to deviate from the standard, and the signing of an acceptance does not *preclude* such departures; however, such signature indicates an *intention* to follow the commercial standard where practicable, in the production, distribution, or consumption of the article in question.

18. The advantage which may be gained from the establishment of commercial standards is dependent upon the

   A. degree of consumer and manufacturer acceptance
   B. improvement of product quality
   C. degree of change required in the manufacturing process
   D. establishment and use of the highest standards

19. Nationally respected and adopted commercial standards are

   A. *undesirable;* as they are a direct benefit to unscrupulous manufacturers
   B. *desirable;* as they serve as a yardstick for consumers
   C. *undesirable;* as they tend to lower quality
   D. *desirable;* as they tend to reduce manufacturing costs

20. The word *preclude,* as used in this paragraph, means MOST NEARLY 20._____

    A. permit B. allow C. include D. prevent

21. The word *intention,* as used in this paragraph, means MOST NEARLY 21._____

    A. agreement B. impulse C. objection D. obstinance

22. The word *recognized,* as used in this paragraph, means MOST NEARLY 22._____

    A. desirable B. stable C. branded D. accepted

23. The word *criteria,* as used in this paragraph, means MOST NEARLY 23._____

    A. efforts B. standards C. usage D. costs

Questions 24-25.

DIRECTIONS: Questions 24 and 25 are to be answered in accordance with the paragraph below.

Sewage treatment plants are designed so that the sewage flow reaches the plant by gravity. In some instances, a small percentage of the sewerage system may be below the planned level of the plant. Economy in construction and other factors may indicate that the raising of that lower portion of the flow by means of pumps, to the desired plant elevation, is more desirable than lowering the plant structure. Some plants operate with this feature.

24. According to the above paragraph, 24._____

    A. a small percentage of the sewage reaches the plant by means of gravity
    B. all sewage reaches the plant by means of gravity
    C. where sewage cannot reach the plant by gravity, it is pumped
    D. pumping is used so that all sewage can reach the plant

25. According to the above paragraph, the reason that some plants are built above the level of the sewerage system is that 25._____

    A. these plants operate more efficiently this way
    B. gravity will naturally bring the sewage in at a lower level
    C. pumping of the sewage is more expensive
    D. these plants are cheaper to build this way

KEY (CORRECT ANSWERS)

1. D
2. A
3. A
4. B
5. C

6. D
7. C
8. C
9. D
10. B

11. C
12. D
13. A
14. D
15. B

16. D
17. A
18. A
19. B
20. D

21. A
22. D
23. B
24. B
25. D

ARITHMETICAL REASONING
EXAMINATION SECTION
TEST 1

DIRECTIONS: Each question or incomplete statement is followed by several suggested answers or completions. Select the one that BEST answers the question or completes the statement. *PRINT THE LETTER OF THE CORRECT ANSWER IN THE SPACE AT THE RIGHT.*

1.

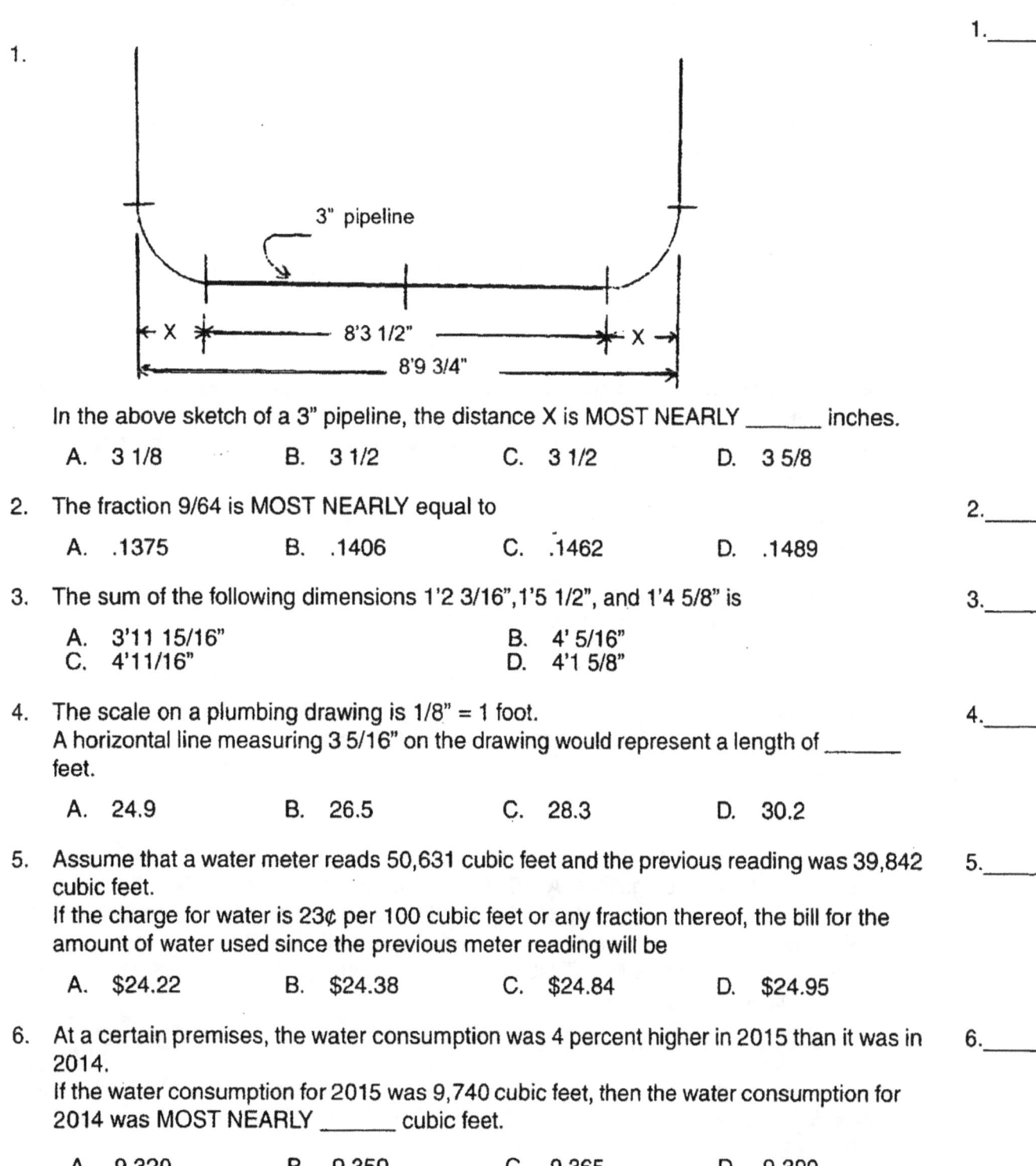

In the above sketch of a 3" pipeline, the distance X is MOST NEARLY _____ inches.

A. 3 1/8   B. 3 1/2   C. 3 1/2   D. 3 5/8

2. The fraction 9/64 is MOST NEARLY equal to

A. .1375   B. .1406   C. .1462   D. .1489

3. The sum of the following dimensions 1'2 3/16", 1'5 1/2", and 1'4 5/8" is

A. 3'11 15/16"   B. 4' 5/16"
C. 4'11/16"   D. 4'1 5/8"

4. The scale on a plumbing drawing is 1/8" = 1 foot.
A horizontal line measuring 3 5/16" on the drawing would represent a length of _____ feet.

A. 24.9   B. 26.5   C. 28.3   D. 30.2

5. Assume that a water meter reads 50,631 cubic feet and the previous reading was 39,842 cubic feet.
If the charge for water is 23¢ per 100 cubic feet or any fraction thereof, the bill for the amount of water used since the previous meter reading will be

A. $24.22   B. $24.38   C. $24.84   D. $24.95

6. At a certain premises, the water consumption was 4 percent higher in 2015 than it was in 2014.
If the water consumption for 2015 was 9,740 cubic feet, then the water consumption for 2014 was MOST NEARLY _____ cubic feet.

A. 9,320   B. 9,350   C. 9,365   D. 9,390

7. A pump delivers water at a constant rate of 40 gallons per minute.
   If there are 7.5 gallons to a cubic foot of water, the time it will take to fill a tank 6 feet x 5 feet x 4 feet is MOST NEARLY _____ minutes.

   A. 15   B. 22.5   C. 28.5   D. 30

8. The total weight, in pounds, of three lengths of 3" cast-iron pipe 7'6" long, weighing 14.5 pounds per foot, and four lengths of 4" cast-iron pipe each 5'0" long, weighing 13.0 pounds per foot, is MOST NEARLY

   A. 540   B. 585   C. 600   D. 665

9. The water pressure at the bottom of a column of water 34 feet high is 14.7 lbs./sq.in. The water pressure in lbs./sq.in. at the bottom of the column of water 12 feet high is MOST NEARLY

   A. 3   B. 5   C. 7   D. 9

10. The number of cubic yards of earth that would be removed when digging a trench 8 feet wide x 9 feet deep x 63 feet long is

    A. 56   B. 168   C. 314   D. 504

11. On test, a meter registered one cubic foot for each 1 1/3 cubic feet of water that passed through it.
    If the meter had a reading of 1,200 cubic feet, we may conclude that the CORRECT amount should be _____ cubic feet.

    A. 800   B. 900   C. 1,500   D. 1,600

12. A water use meter reads 87,463 cubic feet.
    If the previous reading was 17,377 cubic feet and the rate charged is 15 cents per 100 cubic feet, the bill for water use during this period is about

    A. $45.00   B. $65.00   C. $85.00   D. $105.00

13. Under proper conditions, the one of the following groups of pipes that gives the same flow in gals/min as one 6" diameter pipe is (neglect friction) _____ pipes of _____ diameter each.

    A. 3; 3"   B. 4; 3"   C. 2; 4"   D. 3; 4"

14. A roof tank is used to furnish the domestic water supply to a ten story building. This tank has a capacity of 5,900 gallons. At 10:00 A.M. one morning, the tank is half full.
    If water is being used at the rate of 50 gals/min, the pump which is used to fill the tank has a rated capacity of 90 gals/min, the time it would take to fill the tank under these conditions is MOST NEARLY _____ hour(s), _____ minutes.

    A. 2; 8   B. 1; 14   C. 2; 32   D. 1; 2

15. The number of gallons of water contained in a cylindrical swimming pool 8 feet in diameter and filled to a depth of 3 feet 6 inches is MOST NEARLY (assume 7.5 gallons = 1 cubic foot)

    A. 30   B. 225   C. 1,320   D. 3,000

16. The charge for metered water is 52 1/2 cents per hundred cubic feet, with a minimum charge of $21 per annum. Of the following, the SMALLEST water usage in hundred cubic feet that would result in a charge GREATER than the minimum is

    A. 39 B. 40 C. 41 D. 42

17. The annual frontage rent on a one-story building 40 ft. in length is $735.00. For each additional story, $52.50 per annum is added to the frontage rent. For demolition, the charge for wetting down is 3/8 of the annual frontage charge.
    The charge for wetting down a building six stories in height, with a 40 ft. frontage, is MOST NEARLY

    A. $369 B. $371 C. $372 D. $374

18. If the drawing of a piping layout is made to a scale of 1/4" equals one foot, then a 7'9" length of piping would be represented by a scaled length on the drawing of APPROXIMATELY _____ inches.

    A. 2 B. 7 3/4 C. 23 1/4 D. 31

19. A plumbing sketch is drawn to a scale of eighth-size. A line measuring 3" on the sketch would be equivalent to _____ feet.

    A. 2 B. 6 C. 12 D. 24

20. If 500 feet of pipe weighs 800 lbs., the number of pounds that 120 feet will weigh is MOST NEARLY

    A. 190 B. 210 C. 230 D. 240

21. If a trench is excavated 3'0" wide by 5'6" deep and 50 feet long, the total number of cubic yards of earth removed is MOST NEARLY

    A. 30 B. 90 C. 150 D. 825

22. Assume that a plumber earns $86,500 per year.
    If eighteen percent of his pay is deducted for taxes and social security, his net weekly pay will be APPROXIMATELY

    A. $1,326 B. $1,365 C. $1,436 D. $1,457.50

23. Assume that a plumbing installation is made up of the following fixtures and groups of fixtures: 12 bathroom groups each containing one W.C., one lavatory, and one bathtub with shower; 12 bathroom groups each containing one W.C., one lavatory, one bathtub, and one shower stall; 24 combination kitchen fixtures; 4 floor drains; 6 slop sinks without flushing rim; and 2 shower stalls (or shower bath).
    The total number of fixtures for the above plumbing installation is MOST NEARLY

    A. 60 B. 95 C. 120 D. 210

24. A triangular opening in a wall forms a 30-60 degree right triangle.
    If the longest side measures 12'0", then the shortest side will measure

    A. 3'0" B. 4'0" C. 6'0" D. 8'0"

25. You are directed to cut 4 pieces of pipe, one each of the following length: 2'6 1/4", 3'9 3/8", 4'7 5/8", and 5'8 7/8".
The total length of these 4 pieces is

   A. 15'7 1/4"   B. 15'9 3/8"   C. 16'5 7/8"   D. 16'8 1/8"

KEY (CORRECT ANSWERS)

1. A
2. B
3. B
4. B
5. C

6. C
7. B
8. B
9. B
10. B

11. D
12. D
13. B
14. B
15. C

16. C
17. D
18. A
19. A
20. A

21. A
22. B
23. C
24. C
25. D

SOLUTIONS TO PROBLEMS

1. 8'3 1/2" + x + x = 8'9 3/4" Then, 2x = 6 1/4", so x = 3 1/8"

2. 9/64 = .140625 = .1406

3. 1'2 3/16" + 1'5 1/2" +1'4 5/8" = 3'11 21/16" = 4'5/16"

4. 3 5/16" ÷ 1/8" =53/16 x 8/1 = 26.5. Then, (26.5)(1 ft.) = 26.5 feet

5. 50,631 - 39,842 = 10,789; 10,789 ÷ 100 = 107.89
   Since the cost is .23 per 100 cubic feet or any fraction thereof, the cost will be
   (.23)(107) + .23 = $24.84

6. 9740 ÷ 1.04 = 9365 cu.ft.

7. 40 ÷ 7.5 = 5 1/3 cu.ft. of water per minute. The volume = (6)(5)(4) = 120 cu.ft. Thus, the number of minutes needed to fill the tank is 120 ÷ 5 1/3 = 22.5

8. 3" pipe: 3 x 7'6" = 22 1/2' x 14.5 lbs. = 326.25
   4" pipe: 4 x 5' = 20' x 13 lbs. = 260
   326.25 + 260 = 586.25 (most nearly 585)

9. Let x = pressure. Then, 34/12 = 14.7/x. So, 34x = 176.4
   Solving, x ≈ 5 lbs./sq.in.

10. (8)(9)(63) = 4536 cu.ft. Since 1 cu.yd. = 27 cu.ft., 4536 cu.ft. is equivalent to 168 cu.yds.

11. Let x = correct amount. Then, $\frac{1}{1200} = \frac{1\frac{1}{3}}{x}$. Solving, x = 1600

12. 87,463 - 17,377 = 70,086; and 70,086 ÷ 100 = 700.86 ≈ 700 Then, (700)(.15) = $105.00

13. Cross-sectional area of a 6" diameter pipe = (π)(3")^2 = 9π sq. in. Note that the combined cross-sectional areas of four 3" diameter pipes = (4)(π)(1.5")^2 = 9π sq. in.

14. 90 - 50 = 40 gals/min. Then, 2950 ÷ 40 = 73.75 min. ≈ 1 hr. 14 min.

15. Volume = (π)(4)^2(3 1/2) = 56π cu.ft. Then, (56π)(7.5) = 1320 gals.

16. For 4100 cu.ft., the charge of (.525)(41) = $21,525 > $21

17. Rent = $73,500 + (5)($52.50) = $997,50. For demolition, the charge = (3/8)($997.50) $374

18. (1/4")(7.75) = 2"

19. (3")(8) = 24" = 2 ft.

6 (#1)

20. Let x = weight. Then, 500/800 = 120/x . Solving, x = 192 190 lbs.

21. (3')(5 1/2')(50') = 825 cu.ft. Then, 825 ÷ 27 ≈ 30 cu.yds.

22. Net pay = (.82)($86,500) = $70,930/yr. Weekly pay = $70,930 ÷ 52 ≈ $1365

23. (12x3) + (12x4) +24+4+6+2= 120

24. The shortest side = (1/2)(hypotenuse) = (1/2)(12') = 6'

25. 2'6 1/4" + 3'9 3/8" + 4'7 5/8" + 5'8 7/8 " = 14'30 17/8" = 16'8 1/8"

TEST 2

DIRECTIONS: Each question or incomplete statement is followed by several suggested answers or completions. Select the one that BEST answers the question or completes the statement. *PRINT THE LETTER OF THE CORRECT ANSWER IN THE SPACE AT THE RIGHT.*

1. The sum of the following pipe lengths, 15 5/8", 8 3/4", 30 5/16" and 20 1/2", is 1.____
   A. 77 1/8" B. 76 3/16" C. 75 3/16" D. 74 5/16"

2. If the outside diameter of a pipe is 6 inches and the wall thickness is 1/2 inch, the inside area of this pipe, in square inches, is MOST NEARLY 2.____
   A. 15.7 B. 17.3 C. 19.6 D. 23.8

3. Three lengths of pipe 1'10", 3'2 1/2", and 5'7 1/2", respectively, are to be cut from a pipe 14'0" long. 3.____
   Allowing 1/8" for each pipe cut, the length of pipe remaining is
   A. 3'1 1/8" B. 3'2 1/2" C. 3'3 1/4" D. 3'3 5/8"

4. According to the building code, the MAXIMUM permitted surface temperature of combustible construction materials located near heating equipment is 76.5°C. (°F=(°Cx9/5)+32) 4.____
   Maximum temperature Fahrenheit is MOST NEARLY
   A. 170° F B. 195° F C. 210° F D. 220° F

5. A pump discharges 7.5 gals/minutes. 5.____
   In 2.5 hours the pump will discharge _____ gallons.
   A. 1125 B. 1875 C. 1950 D. 2200

6. A pipe with an outside diameter of 4" has a circumference of MOST NEARLY _____ inches. 6.____
   A. 8.05 B. 9.81 C. 12.57 D. 14.92

7. A piping sketch is drawn to a scale of 1/8" = 1 foot. 7.____
   A vertical steam line measuring 3 1/2" on the sketch would have an ACTUAL length of _____ feet.
   A. 16 B. 22 C. 24 D. 28

8. A pipe having an inside diameter of 3.48 inches and a wall thickness of .18 inches will have an outside diameter of _____ inches. 8.____
   A. 3.84 B. 3.64 C. 3.57 D. 3.51

9. A rectangular steel bar having a volume of 30 cubic inches, a width of 2 inches, and a height of 3 inches will have a length of _____ inches. 9.____
   A. 12 B. 10 C. 8 D. 5

10. A pipe weighs 20.4 pounds per foot of length. 10.____
    The total weight of eight pieces of this pipe with each piece 20 feet in length is MOST NEARLY _____ pounds.
    A. 460 B. 1,680 C. 2,420 D. 3,260

115

11. Assume that four pieces of pipe measuring 2'1 1/4", 4'2 3/4", 5'1 9/16", and 6'3 5/8", respectively, are cut with a saw from a pipe 20"0" long.
Allowing 1/16" waste for each cut, the length of the remaining pipe is

    A. 2'1 9/16"   B. 2'2 9/16"   C. 2'4 13/16"   D. 2'8 9/16"

12. If one cubic inch of steel weighs 0.28 pounds, the weight, in pounds, of a steel bar 1/2" x 6" x 2'0" long is MOST NEARLY

    A. 11   B. 16   C. 20   D. 24

13. If the circumference of a circle is equal to 31.416 inches, then its diameter, in inches, is equal to MOST NEARLY

    A. 8   B. 9   C. 10   D. 13

14. Assume that a steam fitter's helper receives a salary of $171.36 a day for 250 days is considered a full work year. If taxes, social security, hospitalization, and pension deducted from his salary amounts to 16 percent of his gross pay, then his net yearly salary will be MOST NEARLY

    A. $31,788   B. $35,982   C. $41,982   D. $42,840

15. If the outside diameter of a pipe is 14 inches and the wall thickness is 1/2 inch, then the inside area of the pipe, in square inches, is MOST NEARLY

    A. 125   B. 133   C. 143   D. 154

16. A steam leak in a pipe line allows steam to escape at a rate of 50,000 pounds each month.
Assuming that the cost of steam is $2.50 per 1,000 pounds, the TOTAL cost of wasted steam from this leak for a 12-month period would amount to

    A. $125   B. $300   C. $1,500   D. $3,000

17. If 250 feet of 4" pipe weighs 400 pounds, the weight of this pipe per linear foot is _____ pounds.

    A. 1.25   B. 1.50   C. 1.60   D. 1.75

18. A set of heating plan drawings is drawn to a scale of 1/4" = 1 foot.
If a length of pipe measures 4 5/8" on the drawing, the ACTUAL length of the pipe, in feet, is

    A. 16.3   B. 16.8   C. 17.5   D. 18.5

19. The TOTAL length of four pieces of pipe whose lengths are 3'4 1/2", 2'1 5/16", 4'9 3/8", and 2'3 1/4", respectively, is

    A. 11'5 7/16"   B. 11'6 7/16"
    C. 12'5 7/16"   D. 12'6 7/16"

20. Assume that a pipe trench is 3 feet wide, 3 feet deep, and 300 feet long.
If the unit cost of excavating the trench is $120 per cubic yard, the TOTAL cost of excavating the trench is

    A. $1,200   B. $12,000   C. $27,000   D. $36,000

21. The TOTAL length of four pieces of 1 1/2" galvanized steel pipe whose lengths are 7 ft. + 3 1/2 inches, 4 ft. + 2 1/4 inches, 6 ft. + 7 inches, and 8 ft. +5 1/8 inches is

    A. 26 feet + 5 7/8 inches
    B. 25 ft. + 6 7/8 inches
    C. 25 feet + 4 1/4 inches
    D. 25 ft. + 3 3/8 inches

21._____

22. A swimming pool is 25' wide by 75' long and has an average depth of 5'. 1 cubic foot contains 7.5 gallons of water. The capacity, when filled to the overflow, is _____ gallons.

    A. 9,375   B. 65,625   C. 69,005   D. 70,312

22._____

23. The sum of 3 1/4, 5 1/8, 2 1/2 , and 3 3/8 is

    A. 14   B. 14 1/8   C. 14 1/4   D. 14 3/8

23._____

24. Assume that it takes 6 men 8 days to do a particular job. If you have only 4 men available to do this job and they all work at the same speed, then the number of days it would take to complete the job would be

    A. 11   B. 12   C. 13   D. 14

24._____

25. The total length of four pieces of 2" O.D. pipe, whose lengths are 7'3 1/2", 4'2 3/16", 5'7 5/16", and 8'5 7/8", respectively, is MOST NEARLY

    A. 24'6 3/4"
    B. 24'7 15/16"
    C. 25'5 13/16"
    D. 25'6 7/8"

25._____

KEY (CORRECT ANSWERS)

1.	C	11.	B
2.	C	12.	C
3.	D	13.	C
4.	A	14.	B
5.	A	15.	B
6.	C	16.	C
7.	D	17.	C
8.	A	18.	D
9.	D	19.	D
10.	D	20.	B

21. A
22. D
23. C
24. B
25. D

SOLUTIONS TO PROBLEMS

1. 15 5/8" + 8 3/4" + 30 5/16" + 20 1/2" = 73 35/16" = 75 3/16"

2. Inside diameter = 6" - 1/2" - 1/2" = 5". Area = $(\pi)(5/2")^2 \approx$ 19.6 sq. in.

3. Pipe remaining = 14' - 1'10" - 3'2 1/2" - 5'7 1/2" - (3)(1/8") = 3'3 5/8"

4. 76.5 x 9/5 = 137.7 + 32 = 169.7

5. 7.5 x 150 = 1125

6. Radius = 2" Circumference = $(2\pi)(2") \approx$ 12.57"

7. 3 1/2" 1/8" = (7/2)(8/1) = 28 Then, (28)(1 ft.) = 28 feet

8. Outside diameter = 3.48" + .18" + .18" = 3.84"

9. 30 = (2)(3)(length). So, length = 5"

10. Total weight = (20.4)(8)(20) $\approx$ 3260 lbs.

11. 20' - 2'1 1/4" - 4'2 3/4" - 5'1 9/16" - 6'3 5/8" - (4)(1/16") = 2'2 9/16"

12. Weight = (.28)(1/2")(6")(24") = 20.16 $\approx$ 20 lbs.

13. Diameter = 31.416" $\div \pi \approx$ 10"

14. His net pay for 250 days = (.84)($171.36)(250) = $35,985.60 $\approx$ $35,928 (from answer key)

15. Inside diameter = 14" - 1/2" - 1/2" = 13". Area = $(\pi)(13/2")^2 \approx$ 133 sq.in

16. (50,000 lbs.)(12) = 600,000 lbs. per year. The cost would be ($2.50)(600) = $1500

17. 400 $\div$ 250 = 1.60 pounds per linear foot

18. 4 5/8" $\div$ 1/4" = 37/8 . 4/1 = 18.5 Then, (18.5)(1 ft.) = 18.5 feet

19. 3'4 1/2" + 2'1 5/16" + 4'9 3/8" + 2'3 1/4" = 11'17 23/16" = 12'6 7/16"

20. (3')(3')(300') = 2700 cu.ft., which is 2700 $\div$ 27 = 100 cu.yds. Total cost = ($120)(100) = $12,000

21. 7'3 1/2" + 4'2 1/4" + 6'7" + 8'5 1/8" = 25'17 7/8" = 26'5 7/8"

22. (25)(75)(5) = 9375 cu.ft. Then, (9375)(7.5) $\approx$ 70,312 gals.

23. 3 1/4 + 5 1/8 + 2 1/2 + 3 3/8 = 13 10/8 = 14 1/4

24. (6) (8) = 48 man-days. Then, 48 $\div$ 4 = 12 days

25. 7'3 1/2" + 4'2 3/16" + 5'7 5/16" + 8'5 7/8"= 24'17 30/16" = 25'6 7/8"

TEST 3

DIRECTIONS: Each question or incomplete statement is followed by several suggested answers or completions. Select the one that BEST answers the question or completes the statement. *PRINT THE LETTER OF THE CORRECT ANSWER IN THE SPACE AT THE RIGHT.*

1. The time required to pump 2,500 gallons of water out of a sump at the rate of 12 1/2 gallons per minutes would be _____ hour(s) _____ minutes. 1._____

   A. 1; 40   B. 2; 30   C. 3; 20   D. 6; 40

2. Copper tubing which has an inside diameter of 1 1/16" and a wall thickness of .095" has an outside diameter which is MOST NEARLY _____ inches. 2._____

   A. 1 5/32   B. 1 3/16   C. 1 7/32   D. 1 1/4

3. Assume that 90 gallons per minute flow through a certain 3-inch pipe which is tapped into a street main. 3._____
   The amount of water which would flow through a 1-inch pipe tapped into the same street main is MOST NEARLY _____ gpm.

   A. 90   B. 45   C. 30   D. 10

4. The weight of a 6 foot length of 8-inch pipe which weighs 24.70 pounds per foot is _____ lbs. 4._____

   A. 148.2   B. 176.8   C. 197.6   D. 212.4

5. If a 4-inch pipe is directly coupled to a 2-inch pipe and 16 gallons per minute are flowing through the 4-inch pipe, then the flow through the 2-inch pipe will be _____ gallons per minute. 5._____

   A. 4   B. 8   C. 16   D. 32

6. If the water pressure at the bottom of a column of water 34 feet high is 14.7 pounds per square inch, the water pressure at the bottom of a column of water 18 feet high is MOST NEARLY _____ pounds per square inch. 6._____

   A. 8.0   B. 7.8   C. 7.6   D. 7.4

7. If there are 7 1/2 gallons in a cubic foot of water and if water flows from a hose at a constant rate of 4 gallons per minute, the time it should take to COMPLETELY fill a tank of 1,600 cubic feet capacity with water from that hose is _____ hours. 7._____

   A. 300   B. 150   C. 100   D. 50

8. Each of a group of fifteen water meter readers read an average of 62 water meters a day in a certain 5-day work week. A total of 5,115 meters are read by this group the following week. 8._____
   The TOTAL number of meters read in the second week as compared to the first week shows a

   A. 10% increase   B. 15% increase
   C. 20% increase   D. 5% decrease

119

9. A certain water consumer used 5% more water in 1994 than he did in 1993. If his water consumption for 1994 was 8,375 cubic feet, the amount of water he consumed in 1993 was MOST NEARLY _____ cubic feet.

   A. 9,014　　B. 8,816　　C. 7,976　　D. 6,776

10. Assume that a water meter reads 40,175 cubic feet and that the previous reading was 29,186 cubic feet.
    If the charge for water is 92 cents per 100 cubic feet or any fraction thereof, the bill for the amount of water used since the previous meter reading should be

    A. $100.28　　B. $101.04　　C. $101.08　　D. $101.20

11. A leaking faucet caused a loss of 216 cubic feet of water in a 30-day month.
    If there are 7.5 gallons in a cubic foot of water, then the AVERAGE loss of water per hour for that month was _____ gallons.

    A. 2 1/4　　B. 2 1/8　　C. 2　　D. 1 3/4

12. The fraction which is equal to .375 is

    A. 3/16　　B. 5/32　　C. 3/8　　D. 5/12

13. A square backyard swimming pool, each side of which is 10 feet long, is filled to a depth of 3 1/2 feet.
    If there are 7 1/2 gallons in a cubic foot of water, the number of gallons of water in the pool is MOST NEARLY _____ gallons.

    A. 46.7　　B. 100　　C. 2,625　　D. 3,500

14. When 1 5/8, 3 3/4, 6 1/3, and 9 1/2 are added, the resulting sum is

    A. 21 1/8　　B. 21 1/6　　C. 21 5/24　　D. 21 1/4

15. When 946 1/2 is subtracted from 1,035 1/4, the result is

    A. 87 1/4　　B. 87 3/4　　C. 88 1/4　　D. 88 3/4

16. When 39 is multiplied by 697, the result is

    A. 8,364　　B. 26,283　　C. 27,183　　D. 28,003

17. When 16.074 is divided by .045, the result is

    A. 3.6　　B. 35.7　　C. 357.2　　D. 3,572

18. To dig a trench 3'0" wide, 50'0" long, and 5'6" deep, the total number of cubic yards of earth to be removed is MOST NEARLY

    A. 30　　B. 90　　C. 140　　D. 825

19. The TOTAL length of four pieces of 2" pipe, whose lengths are 7'3 1/2", 4'2 3/16", 5'7 5/16", and 8'5 7/8", respectively, is

    A. 24'6 3/4"　　　　　　　B. 24'7 15/16"
    C. 25'5 13/16"　　　　　　D. 25'6 7/8"

20. A hot water line made of copper has a straight horizontal run of 150 feet and, when installed, is at a temperature of 45° F. In use, its temperature rises to 190° F. If the coefficient of expansion for copper is 0.0000095" per foot per degree F, the TOTAL expansion, in inches, in the run of pipe is given by the product of 150 multiplied by 0.0000095 by

    A. 145
    B. 145 x 12
    C. 145 divided by 12
    D. 145 x 12 x 12

21. A water storage tank measures 5' long, 4' wide, and 6' deep and is filled to the 5 1/2' mark with water.
    If one cubic foot of water weighs 62 pounds, the number of pounds of water required to COMPLETELY fill the tank is

    A. 7,440   B. 6,200   C. 1,240   D. 620

22. Assume that a pipe worker earns $83,125.00 per year.
    If seventeen percent of his pay is deducted for taxes, social security, and pension, his net weekly pay will be APPROXIMATELY

    A. $1598.50   B. $1504.00   C. $1453.00   D. $1325.00

23. If eighteen feet of 4" cast iron pipe weighs approximately 390 pounds, the weight of this pipe per lineal foot will be MOST NEARLY _____ lbs.

    A. 19   B. 22   C. 23   D. 25

24. If it takes 3 men 11 days to dig a trench, the number of days it will take 5 men to dig the same trench, assuming all work is done at the same rate of speed, is MOST NEARLY

    A. 6 1/2   B. 7 3/4   C. 8 1/4   D. 8 3/4

25. If a trench is dug 6'0" deep, 2'6" wide, and 8'0" long, the area of the opening, in square feet, is MOST NEARLY

    A. 48   B. 32   C. 20   D. 15

KEY (CORRECT ANSWERS)

1.	C	11.	A
2.	D	12.	C
3.	D	13.	C
4.	A	14.	C
5.	B	15.	D
6.	B	16.	C
7.	D	17.	C
8.	A	18.	A
9.	C	19.	D
10.	D	20.	A

21. D
22. D
23. B
24. A
25. C

SOLUTIONS TO PROBLEMS

1. 2500 ÷ 12 1/2 = 200 min. = 3 hrs. 20 min.

2. 1 1/16" + .095" + .095" = 1.0625 + .095 + .095 = 1.2525" ≈ 1 1/4"

3. Cross-sectional areas for a 3-inch pipe and a 1-inch pipe are $(\pi)(1.5)^2$ and $(\pi)(.5)^2$ = 2.25 π and .25 π, respectively. Let x = amount of water flowing through the 1-inch pipe. Then, $\frac{90}{x} = \frac{2.25\pi}{.25\pi}$. Solving, x = 10 gals/min

4. (24.70)(6) = 148.2 lbs.

5. $\frac{4" \text{ pipe}}{16 \text{ gallons}} = \frac{2" \text{ pipe}}{x \text{ gallons}}$, 4x = 32, x = 8

6. Let x = pressure. Then, 34/18 = 14.7/x. Solving, x ≈ 7.8

7. (1600)(7.5) = 12,000 gallons. Then, 12,000 ÷ 4 = 3000 min. = 50 hours

8. (15)(62)(5) = 4650. Then, (5115-4650)/4650 = 10% increase

9. 8375 ÷ 1.05 ≈ 7976 cu.ft.

10. 40,175 - 29,186 = 10,989 cu.ft. Then, 10,989 100 = 109.89. Since .92 is charged for each 100 cu.ft. or fraction thereof, total cost = (.92)(110) = $101.20

11. (216)(7.5) = 1620 gallons. In 30 days, there are 720 hours. Thus, the average water loss per hour = 1620 ÷ 720 = 2 1/4 gallons.

12. .375 = 375/1000 = 3/8

13. Volume = (10)(10)(3 1/2) = 350 cu.ft. Then, (350)(7 1/2) = 2625 gallons

14. 1 5/8 + 3 3/4 + 6 1/3 + 9 1/2 = 19 53/24 = 21 5/24

15. 1035 1/4 - 946 1/2 = 88 3/4

16. (39)(697) = 27,183

17. 16.074 .045 = 357.2

18. (3')(50')(5 1/2') = 825 cu.ft. ≈ 30 cu.yds., since 1 cu.yd. = 27 cu.ft.

19. 7'3 1/2" + 4'2 3/16" + 5'7 5/16" + 8'5 7/8" = 24'17 30/16" = 25'6 7/8"

20. Total expansion = (150)(.0000095)(145)

21. Number of pounds needed = (5)(4)(6-5 1/2)(62) = 620

22. Net annual pay = ($83,125)(.83) ≈ $69000. Then, the net weekly pay = $69000 ÷ 52 ≈ $1325 (actually about $1327)

23. 390 lbs. ÷ 18 = 21.6 lbs. per linear foot

24. (3)(11) = 33 man-days. Then, 33 ÷ 5 = 6.6 ≈ 6 1/2 days

25. Area = (8')(2 1/2') = 20 sq.ft.

ARITHMETIC OF SEWAGE TREATMENT

The English system of measurements is used for computations at sewage treatment works, except in the case of a few determinations. The metric system will be mentioned where the metric units are used.

Basic Units

Linear	1 inch (in.)	= 2.540 centimeters (cm)
	1 foot (ft.)	= 12 inches (in.)
	1 yard (yd.)	= 3 feet (ft.)
	1 mile	= 5,280 feet
	1 meter (m)	= 39.37 in. = 3.281 ft.
		= 1.094 yd.
	1 meter	= 100 centimeters
Area	1 square foot (sq. ft.)	= 144 square inches (sq. in.)
	1 square yard (sq. yd.)	= 9 sq. ft.
	1 acre	= 43,560 sq. ft.
	1 square mile	= 640 acres
Volume	1 cubic foot	= 1728 cubic inches (cu. in.)
	1 cubic yard	= 27 cu. ft.
	1 cubic foot	= 7.48 gallons
	1 gallon (gal.)	= 231 cu. in.
	1 gallon	= 4 quarts (qt)
	1 gallon	= 3.785 liters(1)
	1 liter	= 1000 milliliters (ml)
Weight	1 pound (lb.)	= 16 ounces = 7000 grains
		= 453.6 grams
	1 ounce	= 28.35 grams (g)
	1 kilogram	= 1000 grams
	1 gram	=1000 milligrams (mg)
	1 cu. ft. water	= 62.4 pounds
	1 gallon water	= 8.33 pounds
	1 liter water	= 1 kilogram
	1 milliliter water	= 1 gram

Definition of Terms

A *ratio* is the indicated division of two pure numbers. As such is indicates the relative magnitude of two quantities. The ratio of 2 to 3 is written 2/3.

A *pure* number is used without reference to any particular thing.

A *concrete* number applies to a particular thing and is the product of a pure number and a physical unit. 5 ft. means 5 times 1 ft. or 5 X (1 ft.).

Rate units are formed when one physical unit is divided by another.

$$\frac{60 \text{ft.}}{2 \text{sec.}} = 30 \frac{(\text{ft.})}{(\text{sec.})}$$

Physical units can be formed by multiplying two or more other physical units.

1 ft. X 1 ft. = 1 ft. X ft. = 1 ft.^{2} (square foot)

Physical units may cancel each other.

$$\frac{6 \text{ ft} \times 7.48 \text{ gallons}}{1 \text{ ft.}} = 6 \times 7.48 \text{ gallons}$$

Per cent means per 100 and is the numerator of a fraction whose denominator is always 100. It may be expressed by the symbol "%". The word *per* refers to a fraction whose numerator precedes *per* and whose denominator follows. Hence "per" means "divided by." It is often indicated by a sloping line as "/."

Problem: What is 15 per cent of 60?

$$60 \times \frac{15}{100} = \frac{900}{100} = 9$$

Problem: One pound of lime is stirred into one gallon of water.

What is the per cent of lime in the slurry?

$$\frac{1}{1+8.33} \times 100 = \frac{100}{1+8.33} = 10.7 \text{ per cent}$$

Formulas

Circumference of a circle = $\Pi D = 2\Pi R$

Area of a circle $= \Pi R^2 = \dfrac{\Pi D^2}{4}$

$\Pi = 3.1416$
Area of triangle = 1/2 base X altitude
Area of rectangle = base X altitude
Cylindrical area = circumference of base X length
Volume of cylinder = area of base X length
Volume of rectangular tank = area of bottom X depth
Volume of cone = 1/3 X area of base X height
Velocity = distance divided by time. Inches, feet, or miles divided by hours, minutes, or seconds.
Discharge = volume of flow divided by time.
Gallons or cubic feet divided by days, hours, minutes, or seconds.
1 cu. ft. per sec. = 647,000 gallons per day.
1 mgd = 1.54 cfs = 92.4 cfm

Detention Time. The theoretical time equals the volume of tank divided by the flow per unit time. The flow volume and tank volume must be in the same units.

$$\frac{20{,}000 \text{ gal}}{200 \dfrac{\text{gal}}{\text{min.}}} = 100 \text{ minutes}$$

Problem: A tank is 60 X 20 X 30 ft. The flow is 5 mgd.

What is the detention time in hours?

1 mgd = 92.4 cfm

$$\frac{60 \text{ ft.} \times 20 \text{ ft.} \times 30 \text{ ft.}}{92.4 \times \dfrac{5 \text{ ft}^3}{\text{min}}} = 78 \text{ min. or 1 hr. and 18 min. or 1.3 hours}$$

Surface Settling Rate:

This means gallons per square foot of tank surface per day.

Problem: If the daily flow is 0.5 mgd and the tank is 50 ft. long and 12 ft. wide, calculate the surface settling rate.

$$\frac{500,000 \text{ gal./day}}{50 \text{ ft.} \times 12 \text{ ft.}} = \frac{833 \text{ gal.}}{\text{ft.}^2 \times \text{day}}$$

Weir Overflow Rate:

This means gallons per day per foot length of weir.

Problem: A circular settling tank is 90 ft. in diameter. The flow is 3.0 mgd. Calculate the weir overflow rate.

$$\frac{3,000,000 \text{ gal./day}}{\Pi \times 90 \text{ ft.}} = \frac{10,600 \text{ gal}}{\text{ft.} \times \text{day}}$$

Rate of Filtration: The mgd is divided by the acres of stone to give

$$\frac{\text{mg}}{\text{acre} \times \text{day}} = \text{mgad}$$

$$\frac{\text{mg}}{\text{acre} \times \text{ft.} \times \text{day}} = \text{mgaftd}$$

An acre-ft. is an acre in area and 1 ft. deep.
A fixed-nozzle filter is 140 × 125 feet. Stone is six feet deep. Flow is 9 mgd. Calculate the rate of dosing or hydraulic loading in mg per acre-foot per day.

$$\frac{140 \times 125}{43560} = \text{acres} = 0.402$$

$$0.402 \times 6 = 2.412 \text{ acre-feet}$$

$$\frac{9}{2.412} = \frac{\text{mg}}{\text{acre} \times \text{ft.} \times \text{day}} = 3.73$$

The BOD of a settling tank effluent is 200 ppm. If 15 lb. of BOD per 1000 ft.^{3} of stone is to be the organic loading, how many cubic feet of stone are necessary with a hydraulic loading of 3 mgd.

$$\frac{200 \times 8.33 \times 3 \times 1000}{15} = 333,333 \text{ ft.}^3$$

$$\frac{333,333}{6} = 55,500 \text{ ft.}^2 \text{ for filter area if stone is 6 ft. deep.}$$

Parts per million:

This is a weight ratio. Any unit may be used; pounds per million pounds or milligrams per liter if the liquid has a specific gravity equal to water or very nearly so. 1 liter of water = 1,000,000 milligrams.

   1 ppm = 8.33 lbs. per million gallons
   1 ppm = 1 milligram per liter

A sewage with 600 ppm suspended solids has 600 X 8.33 = 4998 lb. of suspended solids per million gallons.

Efficiency of Removal:

$$\frac{\text{ppm influent - ppm effluent}}{\text{ppm influent}} \cdot 100 = \text{percent efficiency of removal}$$

Percent of Moisture:

$$\frac{\text{wt. of wet sludge - wt. of day sludge}}{\text{wt. of wet sludge}} \cdot 100 = \text{percent moisture}$$

Percent of Dry solids:

$$\frac{\text{wt. of day sludge}}{\text{wt. of wet sludge}} \cdot 100 = \text{parcent day solids}$$

Other calculated quantities that need no special explanation are:
   Square feet of sludge drying bed per capita
   Cubic feet of digestion space per capita
   Cubic feet of sludge produced per day per capita
   Cubic feet of grit per million gallons
   Pounds of sludge per capita per day
   Cubic feet of gas per capita per day
   Kilowatt-hours per million gallons pumped

Specific Gravity: This is the ratio of the density of a substance to the density of water. There is no unit. Density = the weight of unit volume.

$$S.G. = \frac{(\text{wt. bottle with sludge}) - (\text{wt. of empty bottle})}{(\text{wt. bottle with water}) - (\text{wt. of empty bottle})}$$

1 gallon of water = 8.33 lbs.
1 cu. ft. of water = 62.4 lbs.
These vary slightly with temperature.
   Water at 32° F. = 62.417 lb./ft.^{3}

Water at 62° F. = 62.355 lb./ft.^{3}

Water at 212° F. = 59.7 lb./ft.^{3}

Ice   = 57.5 lb./ft.^{3}

Problem: What is the weight of dry solids in 1000 gallons of 10% sludge whose specific gravity is 1.04?

$$1000 \times 8.33 \times 1.40 \times \frac{10}{100} = 866.3 \text{ lbs.}$$

Mixtures:

If two materials of different percentages are to be mixed to produce an intermediate percentage, it may be done by rectangle method. Problem: We have 30 per cent and 50 per cent material. In what ratio shall they be mixed to produce 37 per cent material.

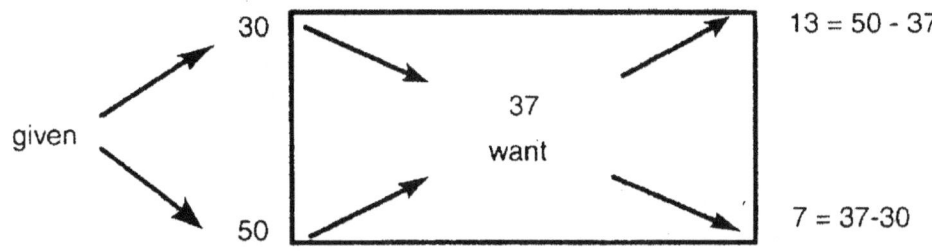

Desired ration is 13 parts of the 30 per cent and 7 parts of the 50 per cent. This will give us 20 parts of 37 per cent.

BASIC FUNDAMENTALS OF WATER QUALITY

TABLE OF CONTENTS

	Page
Reasons for Water Treatment	1
Quality Control Tests	2
Drinking Water Standards	3
Composition of Water from Various Sources	5
Self-Purification and Storage	8
Methods of Water Treatment	10

BASIC FUNDAMENTALS OF WATER QUALITY

Water, if strictly defined in the chemical sense, is H_2O a compound which, like all other pure substances, has a definite and constant composition. Therefore it should, like any pure compound, exhibit predictable chemical and physical characteristics. Indeed, the properties of a pure compound are so dependable that they may be used for identification if an unknown sample is submitted to a laboratory. In other words, water might be expected to be the same, regardless of its origin. In this context, discussing the "quality" of water, or of water from a particular source, would be rather meaningless.

One of the predictable physical properties of this widely distributed compound is a rather remarkable power to dissovle other materials. Familiar as we are with its characteristics, we tend to accept the solvent power of water as a matter of course, and to see nothing remarkable in it. But if water is compared with other known liquids, it is found that none of the others is capable of dissolving so wide a range of compounds of varying compositions. As a result, water seldom if very occurs in nature in a chemically pure state.

In addition to a variety of dissolved materials, water drawn from a natural source usually contains particles of insoluble, or at least undissolved, materials in suspension. The size and the concentration of these suspended particles vary considerably, depending upon the source, from the sand grains sometimes present in rapid, turbulent surface streams to the submicroscopic dispersions known as colloids. Included among the suspended particles, there may be living cells of thousands of different kinds of microorganisms.

Thus, when we speak of the quality of water, our concern is not really with the water itself, but with the other materials present. It is these impurities which determine, to a very large degree, the suitability of a water source for human uses, the problems associated with utilizing it, and the kind and extent of treatment required.

Reasons for Water Treatment

In the broadest possible terms, the objectives of water treatment may be classified under three general headings: (1) to protect the health of the community, (2) to supply a product which is esthetically desirable, and (3) to protect the property of the consumers. Each of these is so broad that it requires further explanation, and each embraces several specific methods of treatment.

Protection of the public health implies first that the treated water must be free of microorganisms capable of causing human disease, and second that the concentrations of any chemical substances which are poisonous or otherwise harmful must be reduced to safe levels. Only rarely do raw water supplies contain significant levels of toxic chemicals. But, more often than not, the microbiological quality of the water requires improvement or protection. In the United States, this aspect of water treatment has progressed to the point that the physiological safety of public water supplies usually is taken for granted. In some parts of the world, it is considered necessary when visiting a strange city to carry a private supply of drinking water, or to inquire whether it is safe to drink the local supply. The situation in the United States, which is unquestionably a credit to the water treatment profession, has permitted increased attention to the other two general objectives mentioned in the previous paragraph.

An esthetically desirable water supply requires that the final product shall be as low as possible in color, turbidity, and suspended solids, as cold as possible, and free from undesirable tastes and odors. Since the subject of tastes and odors is highly subjective, it may be impossible to produce a product which is equally pleasing to all consumers. However, strong, distinctive tastes and odors, as well as those which are disagreeable to a significant percentage of the population, are definitely to be avoided. The esthetic quality of a water supply cannot be completely divorced from the question of public health, since objections to the taste, odor, color, etc. of a perfectly safe public supply may prompt consumers to use water from another source which is more attractive, but which, due to lack of protection, may be considerably more dangerous.

The question of property protection is a broad one, and its specific implications depend upon the purpose for which the water is used. Thus the requirements may, and occasionally do, vary among different consumers using the same supply. For domestic supplies, the usual requirements are that the water shall not be excessively corrosive to plumbing and other metal equipment, that it shall not deposit troublesome quantities of scale, and that it shall not stain porcelain plumbing fixtures. For industrial purposes, the requirements may be even more stringent. For example, more than 10 ppm of chlorides interfere with the manufacture of insulating paper. Generally speaking, public suppliers do not find it practical to meet the strict and sometimes varied requirements of their industrial customers. Instead, they maintain a quality suitable for domestic consumption, and if necessary the industries provide further treatment on their own premises.

Quality Control Tests

In his efforts to maintain the quality of his product, the operator or superintendent of a water treatment plant relies upon various chemical and physical tests. In this way, he accomplishes several purposes. Most importantly, perhaps, he assures himself of his success in meeting the standards which are required and desired. If for any reason the quality temporarily becomes unsatisfactory, the test results advise him of the problem, and permit prompt corrective action. By keeping permanent records of the results, he is in a position to demonstrate the quality of his product to the regulatory authorities, or to any other interested individual or agency.

Tests used for monitoring or controlling water quality are suggested by the objectives listed in the previous section. Few, if any, plants find it necessary to perform all the tests discussed in this manual. Ordinarily, the only tests selected for frequent, regular performance are those pertinent to the quality problems experienced at a particular plant. Other tests may be run less frequently to periodically provide a more complete evaluation of the water quality. Samples of the raw water as well as the treated water are often analyzed, since the former may provide information which is necessary to the control of the treatment plant. In some types of treatment, it is desirable in addition to analyze samples collected at intermediate points. Many suppliers also find it advisable to test samples collected from various parts of the distribution system to assure that the water quality is as acceptable when it reaches the consumer as when it leaves the treatment plant.

Determinations of bacteriological quality are most often based upon measurements of the numbers of "coliform bacteria." Although this group of organisms is not known to cause human disease directly, its presence and survival is considered to indicate the potential presence of disease organisms (pathogens), and consequently the number of coliforms present is strictly regulated. In some plants, the enumeration of coliforms is supplemented by the "total plate count," which is an approximate measurement of the total microbial population of the water, or by determining the numbers of one particular species of the coliform group, *Escherichia coli*.

In the vast majority of plants, especially in the United States, control of the bacteriological quality of the water is accomplished by means of chlorination. Therefore, the determination of residual chlorine in its various forms becomes a most important analysis, even though it may not be rigorously correct to consider it a direct means of monitoring the water quality. Closely related to the measurement of residual chlorine is the determination of chlorine demand, which is currently defined as the difference between the concentration of chlorine added and the concentration remaining after a specified period of time. Measurement of the chlorine demand of the raw water is often essential to successful control of the bacteriological quality of the finished product, particularly if the chlorine demand of the source tends to be variable.

Tests for chemical substances known to be poisonous are not ordinarily conducted routinely unless there is reason to suspect the presence of one or more such materials. If the previous history of the water supply, or other circumstance, indicates the possibility of a problem of this kind, the analytical program should include measurement of the concentration of the offending substance, probably both before and after treatment. Otherwise, tests of this type might be included among those which are performed only periodically.

Among the tests related to the esthetic quality of the water, determinations of color, turbidity, suspended solids, and temperature are important. The measurement of taste and odor, unfortunately, is almost as subjective in the laboratory as in the consumer's home or place of business, notwithstanding various attempts to improve its quantitative aspects. For this reason, some plants, in which taste and odor problems are rare, seldom if ever perform the determinations routinely, but rely upon complaints to advise them of the occurrence of a problem. In other places, less fortunate, where strong or disagreeable tastes and odors are a frequent problem, such tests may be a regular part of the quality control program. In a few instances, specific substances such as sulfides and phenols, which are known to affect taste and odor may be measured. Likewise, the determination of iron and manganese may be included in this group, because excessive quantities of either may affect both taste and color. The measurement of dissolved oxygen is sometimes included too, since the majority of people seem to prefer the flavor of water in which the oxygen content is near saturation.

For domestic purposes, the analyses related to protection of property include those which reveal the tendency of the water to corrode metals or to deposit scale. The important tests in this group are those for pH, acidity, alkalinity, total hardness, and calcium. Sometimes a determination of conductivity and total solids may be included, and under certain circumstances a measurement of the concentration of sulfates is important.

Drinking Water Standards

The U. S. Department of Health, Education, and Welfare, through its agency, the U. S. Public Health Service, has published revised standards for the quality of drinking water. Although the federal Public Health Regulations govern only interstate carriers and certain other specified installations, their standards are widely used as guide by other regulatory agencies. Many of the latter have incorporated the PHS standards wholly or in part into their own rules.

Some of the provisions of the Public Health Service standards are summarized below. It must be noted, however, that the complete report[1] from which this information is abstracted includes a great deal of supplementary material which is important in the interpretation and application of the standards. Therefore, the figures quoted do not apply strictly nor without qualification in all cases.

The standard of bacteriological quality is based upon the number of coliform bacteria present. Detailed sampling and testing procedures are specified, and a complete and fairly elaborate description of the method of evaluation sets forth precisely what results are required of an acceptable supply. In effect, the number of coliform bacteria is limited to not more than one organism per 100 ml of water on the average, with not more than five per cent of the samples tested showing numbers greater than this limit.

In regard to physical properties, the turbidity should be less than five units, the color less than 15 units, and the threshold odor number less than three. If the turbidity standard is satisfied, the suspended solids will not be detectable.

"Recommended" limits of concentration established for a number of chemical substances appear in Table VII. These are not absolute standards. Rather it is suggested that these materials "should not be present in a water supply in excess of the listed concentrations where . . . other more suitable supplies are or can be made available."

TABLE I
RECOMMENDED CONCENTRATION LIMITS

Substance	Maximum Concentration, mg/l
Alkyl Benzene Sulfonate	0.5
Arsenic	0.01
Chloride	250.
Copper	1.
Carbon Chloroform Extract	0.2
Cyanide	0.01
Fluoride	0.8-1.7 (See PHS Standards)
Iron	0.3
Manganese	0.05
Nitrate	45.
Phenols	0.001
Sulfate	250.
Total Dissolved Solids	500.
Zinc	5.

In addition to the recommended standards which appear in Table I, concentration limits for certain constituents are established which may be considered absolute, in that exceeding any one of the limits listed provides grounds for rejecting the supply. These figures appear in Table II.

TABLE II
ABSOLUTE CONCENTRATION LIMITS

Substance	Maximum Concentration, mg/l
Arsenic	0.05
Barium	1.0
Cadmium	0.01
Chromium, Hexavalent	0.05
Cyanide	0.2
Fluoride	See Text
Lead	0.05
Selenium	0.01
Silver	0.05

For Fluoride, both the recommended and absolute limits are related to the climate of the locality in question. For the greatest part of New York State, the recommended optimum is 1.1 mg/l, the recommended upper limit is 1.5 mg/l and the absolute limit is 2.2 mg/l. For a small area in the northern part of the state, the corresponding limits are 1.2, 1.7 and 2.4 mg/l, and in the extreme southeastern part, 1.0, 1.3 and 2.0 mg/l.

Radioactivity is also limited, but the acceptability of a given supply is dependent to some extent upon exposure from other sources. A water supply is unconditionally acceptable in this respect if the content of Radium 226 is less than three micro-micro-curies per liter, the content of Strontium 90 is less than 10 micro-micro-curies per liter, and the gross beta-ray activity is less than one microcurie per liter. If the radioactivity of the water supply exceeds the values stated, then its acceptability is judged on the basis of consideration of other sources of radioactivity in the environment.

Composition of Water from Various Sources

As suggested before, virtually all the water used to supply human requirements has at some time, usually quite recently, fallen to the surface of the earth as rain or some other form of precipitation. At this stage, the quantity of foreign material it contains is likely to be at a minimum. Nevertheless, even rain water is not chemically pure H_2O. Not only does it dissolve the gases of the atmosphere as it falls, but it also collects dust and other solid materials suspended in the air. Since the atmospheric solids depend upon both the composition of the soil below and the materials released into the air from combustion, industrial processes, and other sources, analyses of rain or other forms of precipitation reveal surprising variations. In general, however, rainwater may be expected to be very soft, to be low in total solids and alkalinity, to have a pH value somewhat below neutrality, and to be quite corrosive to many metals. A "typical" analysis, subject to the variations mentioned above, might appear as follows:

Hardness	19	mg/l as $CaCO_3$
Calcium	16	mg/l as $CaCO_3$
Magnesium	3	mg/l as $CaCO_3$
Sodium	6	mg/l as Na
Ammonium	0.8	mg/l as N
Bicarbonate	12	mg/l as $CaCO_3$
Acidity	4	mg/l as $CaCO_3$
Chloride	9	mg/l as Cl
Sulfate	10	mg/l as SO_4
Nitrate	0.1	mg/l as N
pH	6.8	

After the water reaches the surface of the ground, it passes over soil and rock into lakes, streams, and reservoirs, or it percolates through the soil and rock into the ground water. In the process, a great variety of materials may be dissolved or taken into suspension. Consequently, it may be expected that the composition of both the surface waters and the ground water of a given area reflects the geology of the region, that is, the composition of the underlying rock formations and of the soils derived from them. In general, the presence of readily soluble formations near the surface, such as gypsum, rock salt, or the various forms of limestone, produce relatively marked effects upon the waters of the area. On the other hand, in the presence of less soluble formations, such as sandstone or granite, the composition of the water tends to remain more like that of rain. As one might expect, local variations are often considerable and occasionally extreme, both in the concentration of any one constituent and in the proportions of the various materials present. The examples given below should be considered with this in view. They are typical only in that they are not remarkable.

Surface water, in an area in which limestone is an important constituent of the geologic formations, might have a composition similar to the following:

Hardness	120	mg/l as $CaCO_3$
Calcium	80	mg/l as $CaCO_3$
Magnesium	40	mg/l as $CaCO_3$
Sodium & Potassium	19	mg/l as Na
Bicarbonate	106	mg/l as $CaCO_3$
Chloride	23	mg/l as Cl
Sulfate	38	mg/l as SO_4
Nitrate	0.4	mg/l as N
Iron	0.3	mg/l as Fe
Silica	18	mg/l as SiO_2
Carbon Dioxide	4	mg/l as $CaCO_3$
pH	7.8	

In such an area, the ground water often contains more hardness and bicarbonate than the surface waters. This is due in part to the longer period of contact with soil and rock, and in part to the fact that carbon dioxide, contributed by the decomposition of organic matter in the soil, greatly increases the solubility of some of the constituents. The folowing analysis might be considered typical of well or spring water in a limestone area:

Hardness	201	mg/l as $CaCO_3$
Calcium	142	mg/l as $CaCO_3$
Magnesium	59	mg/l as $CaCO_3$
Sodium & Potassium	20	mg/l as Na
Bicarbonate	143	mg/l as $CaCO_3$
Chloride	23	mg/l as Cl
Sulfate	59	mg/l as SO_4
Nitrate	0.06	mg/l as N
Iron	0.18	mg/l as Fe
Silica	12	mg/l as SiO_2
Carbon Dioxide	14	mg/l as $CaCO_3$
pH	7.4	

In areas in which the underlying formations are insoluble, that is, where they consist of sand, sandstone, clay, shale, or igneous rocks, the waters tend to he softer and more acid. In general, their content of most dissolved materials is lower. Acidity, however, may be higher than in hard water areas, since carbon dioxide picked up from the soil is not neutralized. Excepting in some areas of igneous rock, iron also tends to be higher in soft waters, since many of the iron compounds of soils and rocks are dissolved by the acidity of the waters. In many soft water areas, the differences between ground waters and surface waters are not as pronounced as in hard water regions, although many exceptions to this generality could be cited.

A more or less typical analysis of surface water in a region of generally insoluble soils and rocks follows:

Hardness	46	mg/l as $CaCO_3$
Calcium	30	mg/l as $CaCO_3$
Magnesium	16	mg/l as $CaCO_3$
Sodium & Potassium	9	mg/l as Na
Bicarbonate	42	mg/l as $CaCO_3$
Chloride	5	mg/l as Cl
Sulfate	12	mg/l as SO_4

Nitrate	1.5	mg/l as N
Iron	1.1	mg/l as Fe
Silica	30	mg/l as SiO_2

Ground water from a similar region might give analytical results similar to the following:

Hardness	61	mg/l as $CaCO_3$
Calcium	29	mg/l as $CaCO_3$
Magnesium	32	mg/l as $CaCO_3$
Sodium	26	mg/l as Na
Bicarbonate	60	mg/l as $CaCO_3$
Chloride	7	mg/l as Cl
Sulfate	17	mg/l as SO_4
Carbon Dioxide	59	mg/l as $CaCO_3$
PH	6.6	
Iron	1.8	mg/l as Fe

It is worth re-emphasizing that each of the constituents listed in the analyses above may vary over a wide range from place to place.

For example, waters are known with hardness values of less than 10 mg/l, and others have concentrations over 1,000 mg/l. Those quoted have been chosen to represent rather moderate, ordinary values occurring in two distinct types of situations common in the United States. It would be a mistake, however, to expect any water sample to correspond exactly to any one of the analyses given as examples.

Good Quality Water. Since waters from various sources may vary so markedly in composition, one may reasonably question which source should be considered most desirable. The problem has several practical consequences. For example, if a choice exists among several available sources, the final decision may rest upon judgment of their relative quality. Also, when the composition is modified by treatment, the objective is to approach, if not always to attain, the ideal.

The characteristics of "good quality water" are implied in earlier sections of this chapter, which discuss the objectives of water treatment and the standards formally adopted by the U.S. Public Health Service. Reviewing those sections will make it evident that the properties desired are mostly negative. That is, the objectives and standards are directed principally to avoiding undesirable qualities. The properties of " good" water may then be summarized in qualitative terms as follows:

1. Absence of harmful concentrations of poisonous chemical substances
2. Absence of the causative microorganisms and viruses of disease
3. Lowest possible levels of color, turbidity, suspended solids, odor, and taste
4. Lowest possible temperature
5. Minimum corrosivity to metals
6. Least possible tendency to deposit scale
7. Lowest possible content of staining materials, such as iron, manganese, and copper

This may appear to suggest that the ideal water contains the lowest possible quantity of total solids but this is not the case. Extremely soft waters tend to be excessively corrosive to metals, and many persons find them unpalatable. Moreover, they seem to be less effective in removing soap by rinsing than waters containing a little hardness.

Although there has been no formal recognition of a set of analytical values characterizing the "ideal" water, the following would probably be considered generally acceptable as an approximation:

Alkyl Benzene Sulfonate	less than 0.1 mg/l, preferably 0
Arsenic	less than 0.01 mg/l, preferably 0
Barium	less than 1 mg/l, preferably 0
Bicarbonate*	150 mg/l as $CaCO_3$
Cadium	less than 0.01 mg/l, preferably 0
Calcium*	70 mg/l as $CaCO_3$
Carbon Chloroform Extract	less than 0.2 mg/l, preferably 0
Carbon Dioxide*	6 mg/1 as $CaCO_3$
Chloride*	less than 250 mg/l, preferably 0
Chromium, Hexavalent	less than 0.05 mg/l, preferably 0
Coliform Bacteria	less than 1 per 100 ml
Color	less than 15 units, preferably 0
Copper	less than 1 mg/l, preferably 0
Cyanide	less than 0.01 mg/l, preferably 0
Fluoride	approximately 0.9 mg/l (somewhat dependent upon climate)
Hardness*	70 mg/l as $CaCO_3$
Iron	less than 0.1 mg/l, preferably 0
Lead	less than 0.05 mg/l, preferably 0
Magnesium*	preferably 0
Manganese	less than 0.02 mg/l, preferably 0
Nitrate	less than 10 mg/l, preferably 0
pH*	7.8
Phenols	less than 0.001 mg/l, preferably 0
Selenium	less than 0.01 mg/l, preferably 0
Silver	less than 0.05 mg/l, preferably 0
Sodium & Potassium*	37 mg/l as Na
Sulfate*	less than 250 mg/l, preferably 0
Suspended Solids	not detectable
Temperature	33 to 40 degrees Fahrenheit
Threshold Odor Number	less than 3, preferably 0
Total Dissolved Solids	less than 500 mg/l
Turbidity	less than 5 units, preferably 0
Zinc	less than 5 mg/l, preferably 0

*The relationships among calcium, bicarbonate, carbon dioxide, and pH should be such as to minimize scaling and corrosion. In some cases, these concentrations may dictate the most desirable concentrations of sulfate, chloride, magnesium, sodium, and potassium.

Self-Purification and Storage

Nature provides some degree of self-purification for all water that has been polluted or contaminated by the introduction of wastes, whether they originate as domestic sewage, industrial wastes, or drainage from yards, streets, and agricultural areas. The rate at which process occurs depends upon the nature and amount of polluting material as well as the physical, chemical, and biological conditions and characteristics of the water itself. Erroneous ideas are prevalent, however, particularly as to the value of aeration and its effect on flowing water. For instance, statements are sometimes made to the effect that "water will purify itself in flowing seven miles," or that natural aeration occurring at waterfalls and rapids will "oxidize" or kill bacteria. Actually, distance in itself has nothing whatever to do with self-purification in a flowing stream. Neither does aeration have much if any direct effect in killing bacteria. Time is the important factor, together wth proper conditions of temperature, sunlight, velocity of flow and many other complex chemical, physical, and biological characteristics. Quiescent sedimentation in a reservoir for a period of about a month may result generally in purification equivalent to that of filtration. Sluggish flow in a stream for a long distance may accomplish the same results.

The general appearance of a stream provides a useful guide to the degree of pollution. For instance, the bed of the unpolluted portion above sources of wastewaters usually is coated with a greenish brown deposit and green, rooted plants will thrive in protected areas. Just below a point of pollution, chemical and biological changes are evident, such as the gradual disappearance of the green plants. This stretch of the stream has been called the "zone of recent pollution."

Further downstream is the "zone of active decomposition", where the bed of the stream may have black sludge deposits, and a characteristic biological population adapted to a plentiful food supply but a limited oxygen supply. If the degree of pollution is great, the dissolved oxygen of the water may be completely exhausted. This results generally in objectionable conditions, the production of odors and gases, and a turbid gray or black appearance of the water. If, on the other hand, the degree of pollution is moderate and the dissolved oxygen content of the water is sufficient, odors are not produced. This condition results when the dissolved oxygen is replenished from the atmosphere and plant life at a rate faster than it is being used up in oxidation of the polluting material. The presence of rapids, falls, or even swiftly flowing water in this zone is helpful insofar as providing an adequate supply of atmospheric oxygen is concerned, since the rate of reaeration is closely related to the turbulence of the water. It should be noted, however, that a supply of oxygen exceeding the requirements does not accelerate the natural purification processes. Since the time is not shortened, a high flow velocity only means that the distance traveled before purification is complete is increased.

Eventually, unless additional pollution is discharged into the stream, the result is the production of an odorless, humus-like material in the stream bed. If the pollution contained nitrogenous materials, the concentration of nitrates in the water increases. There is restoration of the normal dissolved oxygen content, which favors the growth of green aquatic vegetation. Normal conditions are thus restored in this "zone of recovery," the length and position of which are dependent upon the degree of pollution and the natural conditions outlined above.

Essentially, the same action takes place in a natural lake or in an impounding reservoir, although the "zones" described above may not exist as distinct regions. This is due to the complications which are caused by the lack of currents with definite direction. Furthermore, a considerable amount of vertical mixing may occur due to variations in the density of the water. The changes of density, in turn, are caused by the differences of temperature of the water at the various levels in the lake or reservoir. The vertical mixing takes place continuously, but is most noticeable in the spring and fall when temperature changes are most rapid and mixing consequently most vigorous throughout the entire depth of the water. Very often this "turnover" of a lake or reservoir results in the occurrence of tastes and odors in the water supply, which may be due to changes in the types and numbers of microorganisms present, or to changes in the chemical and physical quality of the water.

In general, self-purification results in the removal of organic matter and the degree depends upon the dilution, the effectiveness of reaeration, sedimentation, and most important, the time interval available for biochemical action. The destruction of bacteria introduced with sewage, however, is controlled by a different set of factors. The rate is controlled by the water temperature, available food supply, the germicidal effect of sunlight, sedimentation, and the consumption of the bacteria as food by protozoa. This action is usually slower than the destruction of organic matter. Hence, bacterial contamination may persist long after the visible evidence of pollution has disappeared. Therefore, the only possible way of determining the influence of storage or of passage along a stream upon the bacteriological quality of the water is to measure bacterial numbers in representative samples of water collected at appropriate points.

Unfortunately, the effects of storage and time are not all beneficial in relation to certain characteristics of water. The results of biochemical purification are, for example, conductive to the growth of algae and other forms of microscopic plant and animal life. Although these organisms may have little if any effect on the health of a community as a result of drinking the water, they are the most common cause of tastes and odors, and generally, additional treatment is needed when they are present.

Methods of Water Treatment

The methods employed in the treatment of water depend, to a large extent, on the purpose for which the supply is to be used and the quality of the water being treated. For domestic use, it is desirable to remove any materials, either in suspension or in solution, which are detrimental to the appearance and esthetic appeal of the water. It is absolutely necessary to remove or kill any detrimental microorganisms, and to remove harmful chemical substances. On the other hand, industrial requirements for water quality vary, depending upon the use. For example, for stream generation the control of scale formation is of paramount importance, while textile mills and paper mills demand freedom from iron and manganese.

In general, the many methods normally employed in water treatment practice usually have as their main objective the reduction of the total quantity of foreign substances in the water. Even when the treatment process involves the addition of certain materials, the end result is usually the removal of more material than has been added. There are cases, however, in which certain constituents are removed by substituting other substances, and in some circumstances the content of certain substances may be increased deliberately, in order to impart certain desirable characteristics to the water.

Sedimentation. Sedimentation is more or less effective in the removal of suspended matter, depending upon the size and the density of the particles to be removed, and the time available for the process. Large or heavy particles are removed in a relatively short time, while a much longer period is required for light or finely divided materials. Some of the very finest such as eroded clay may not be removed even by several days' sedimentation. If the concentration of such "non-settleable" particles is excessive, then sedimentation alone is not an adequate method of treatment, and other means must be employed.

Coagulation. This is the technique of treating the water with certain chemicals for the purpose of collecting non-settleable particles into larger or heavier aggregates which are more readily removed. The resulting clumps of solid material, termed "floc," are removed by sedimentation, filtration, or both.

Filtration. Filtration of the water through sand, anthracite, diatomite, and other fine-grained materials is also capable of removing particulate matter too light or too finely divided to be removed by sedimentation. Filters often follow sedimentation units, so that the larger quantity of relatively coarse material is removed by sedimentation, to avoid rapid clogging of the filters, which in turn remove the particles for which sedimentation is not effective. Fine screens or microstrainers are sometimes used prior to sand filtration.

Disinfection. This broad sense means destroying pathogenic organisms. In the practice of water treatment in the United States, it is usually accomplished by the application of chlorine or certain chlorine compounds. Although many other treatment processes mentioned also have some effect upon the microbial population of the water, disinfection is the only step which is intended specifically for control of the bacteriological quality.

Softening. The removal of the elements which contribute hardness to a water supply, primarily calcium and magnesium is called softening. Many water supplies do not require softening, and in some cases, even though the water is hard, softening is not practiced. When domestic supplies are softened, usually the *lime-soda process* or the *ion-exchange process* is used. In the first, chemicals are added to precipitate calcium as calcium carbonate, and if further softening is required, magnesium is precipitated as magnesium hydroxide. Usually, the process results in a reduction of the total quantity of dissolved solids in the water. In the ion-exchange process, calcium and magnesium salts are converted to sodium salts, and little change in the total dissolved solids results.

Aeration. This may be used for a variety of purposes. Since volatile substances are removed in the process to some extent, and these may include materials which affect the taste and odor of the water, aeration is sometimes employed in connection with taste and odor control. Excessive carbon dioxide can also be removed in this way, and the corrosive effect of some water can be reduced. The removal of carbon dioxide by aeration sometimes also reduces the dosages of chemicals required in subsequent treatment processes. Finally, by supplying dissolved oxygen, aeration is often helpful in the removal of iron.

Iron and manganese removal. Specific processes to remove iron and manganese are employed only in waters which contain sufficient concentrations of these substances to cause persistent problems. A number of different techniques exist, and the choice depends upon the concentration and the chemical nature of the iron and manganese present.

Taste and odor removal. Taste and odor are affected by many of the treatment processes which are employed primarily for other purposes, and therefore, like some other characteristics, do not require special processes for control unless rather unusual problems exist. Which one of the several available processes proves to be most successful depends upon the nature and the concentration of the offending substances. It has been mentioned that some odors are effectively removed by aeration. Others may require either adsorption or oxidation for efficient control.

Corrosion control. This is accomplished in some cases by the removal of excess carbon dioxide (e.g., by aeration). In other cases, alkalinity is added to the water in the form of an alkaline chemical such as sodium carbonate.

Fluoridation. The objective of this process is to attain a concentration of fluoride in the water which imparts to the population the maximum degree of resistance to tooth decay.

www.ingramcontent.com/pod-product-compliance
Lightning Source LLC
Chambersburg PA
CBHW082205300426
44117CB00016B/2679